# Orientation and Form

*To my teachers:*
*Solomon E. Asch, Hans Wallach,*
*and Martin Scheerer*

# Orientation and Form

IRVIN ROCK

*Institute for Cognitive Studies*
*Rutgers University*

ACADEMIC PRESS   New York and London     1973

*A Subsidiary of Harcourt Brace Jovanovich, Publishers*

OPTOMETRY

COPYRIGHT © 1973, BY ACADEMIC PRESS, INC.
ALL RIGHTS RESERVED.
NO PART OF THIS PUBLICATION MAY BE REPRODUCED OR
TRANSMITTED IN ANY FORM OR BY ANY MEANS, ELECTRONIC
OR MECHANICAL, INCLUDING PHOTOCOPY, RECORDING, OR ANY
INFORMATION STORAGE AND RETRIEVAL SYSTEM, WITHOUT
PERMISSION IN WRITING FROM THE PUBLISHER.


ACADEMIC PRESS, INC.
111 Fifth Avenue, New York, New York 10003


*United Kingdom Edition published by*
ACADEMIC PRESS, INC. (LONDON) LTD.
24/28 Oval Road, London NW1


Library of Congress Cataloging in Publication Data

Rock, Irvin.
    Orientation and form.

    Bibliography: p.
    1.  Form perception.    2.   Orientation.    I.    Title.
[DNLM:    1.   Form perception.    2.     Orientation.
3.   Visual perception.     WW103 R 682p 1973]
BF293.R63   1973      152.1'423            72–13618
ISBN 0–12–591250–1


PRINTED IN THE UNITED STATES OF AMERICA

# Contents

# Preface

The common facts of everyday life often pose challenging scientific problems that the average person rarely thinks about. In this monograph I address myself to such a problem: namely, why things look different and are often unrecognizable when they are upside down or, to put the matter more generally, why orientation affects form perception. Everyone knows that this is a fact, but few think of it as a problem.

The problem came into sharp focus for me more than 20 years ago when I realized the Gestalt psychologists had established that the essential information for the perception of form was relational. That a form can be transposed in size and position without altering its perceived shape clearly means that the perceptual system is focusing on the geometrical relationships—the way the parts of a figure relate to one another. As long as these relationships remain unchanged, phenomenal form remains unchanged. But if this is true, why does a transposition in the orientation of a figure so often have such a profound effect on its appearance although there is no change in the internal geometry of the figure?

On and off since then I have been thinking about and experimenting on this problem. It soon became clear that there are several factors at work here, not just one. Since I now feel I have explored these factors as far as one can on a purely psychological level, the time seems appropriate to summarize my work and ideas on the subject.

In this monograph I describe some work that has already been published, and much work that has not. In the case of previously unpublished studies, I have tried either to give enough detail in the text proper to make the experiment fully comprehensible (hopefully, even replicable), or to give this detail in an appendix. A very large number of students have worked with me at one time or another on this problem, some as long ago as the early 1950s, and I have of course learned a good deal from them in the process. References to dissertations and joint publications are given in the text, but in many cases no such written paper was completed. Therefore I list the names of all these individuals here, more or less in the chronological order of their participation in this research, with the hope I am not forgetting anyone: John Urban, Richard Bergman, Walter Heimer, Robin Leaman, Janet Simon, David Begelman, David Koulack, Phyllis Dallek, Josephine Scher, Kay Schick, Phyllis Olshansky, George Steinfeld, Edna Ortof, Celia Erde, Joan Harvey, Sal Pappalardo, Laura Vonèche, Carole Ehleben, Robert Turer, Charles Bebber, Ben Susswein, and Douglas Blewett.

Credits to figures from other sources used in this volume are as follows:

Figure 10a, page 13: From R. Thouless, The experience of "upright" and "upsidedown" in looking at pictures. *Miscellanea Psychologia, Albert Michotte* (Éditeurs de l'Institut Supérior de Philosophie, Louvain). Paris: Libraire Philosophique, Joseph Vrin, 1947. P. 130

Figures 10b and 10c, page 13: From G. Kanizsa, and G. Tampieri, *Nuove osservazioni sull' orniamento retinico percezione.* Trieste: Universita degli Studi di Trieste, 1968.

Figure 11, page 13, Figure 12, page 15, and Figure 59, page 77: From I. Rock, The orientation of forms on the retina and in the environment, *The American Journal of Psychology*, 1956, **69**, 516, 520.

Figure 13, page 19: From I. Rock and R. Leaman, An experimental analysis of visual symmetry. *Acta Psychologica*, 1963, **21**, 171–183.

Figure 37, page 46: Reproduced from I. Rock, *The Nature of Perceptual Adaptation*, Fig. 2-2, New York: Basic Books, 1966. P. 2

Figures 57 and 58, page 75: Reproduced from R. N. Shepard and J. Metzler, Mental rotation of three-dimensional objects. *Science*, 1971, **170**(NO. 3972), 702, Figs. 1 and 2, respectively. Copyright 1971 by the American Association for the Advancement of Science.

Figure 60, page 85: From H. Kopfermann, Psychologische Untersuchungen über die Wirkung zweidimensionaler Darstellungen korperlicher Gebilde. *Psychologische Forschung*, 1930, **13**, 293–364.

Figure 61, page 86, Figure 67, page 120, and Figure 68, page 121: From E. Goldmeier, Similarity in visually perceived forms, *Psychological Issues*, 1972, **8**, Monogr. 29.

Figure 66, page 116: From G. Kanizsa, Margini quasi-percettivi in campi con stimolazione omogenea, *Rivista di Psicologia*, 1955, **49**, 16.

I thank Solomon E. Asch, Fred Attneave, John Ceraso, Morris Eagle, Phillip Liss, Arien Mack, and Carl Zuckerman for reading the manuscript at one stage or another and for their very valuable suggestions concerning it. Over the years research on this topic was supported directly and indirectly by grants from the National Science Foundation and the National Institute of Health, and most recently by a Research Scientist Award from the Public Health Service.

★
★ ★

CHAPTER I

# The Problem

There are various ways in which the orientation of an object can be altered, and generally such changes do *not* affect the object's apparent shape. For example, a figure such as that shown in Fig. 1a can be rotated about a horizontal axis as in Fig. 1b, or about a vertical axis as in Fig. 1c, thereby changing its slope or slant. Nevertheless, in such cases the perceived shape of the figure remains more or less unchanged, and for this reason one speaks of shape constancy. It has been assumed that the observer takes into account the figure's slant or slope in assessing the shape signified by the compressed retinal image.

But if the figure is rotated about a horizontal axis that is perpendicular to the plane of the figure, as shown in Fig. 2, then there generally is a marked change in its appearance, and consequently it is often not recognized. For example, Fig. 3 will not look familiar to the reader, but if he rotates the page 90° clockwise, he will

1

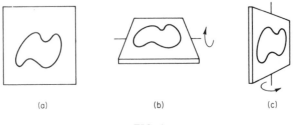

(a)                          (b)                          (c)

**FIG. 1**

undoubtedly recognize it as an outline map of the African continent. Or, to give a different example—one referred to by Ernst Mach (1914)—a square looks quite different when it is rotated 45°, as shown in Fig. 4. In fact, it is no longer even called a square in this position: It is now a diamond.

Other examples of this kind of change in orientation, familiar to everyone, are shown in Figs. 5 and 6. Printed words are harder

**FIG. 2**                               **FIG. 3**

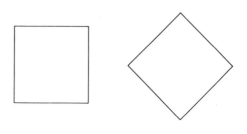

**FIG. 4**

alphabet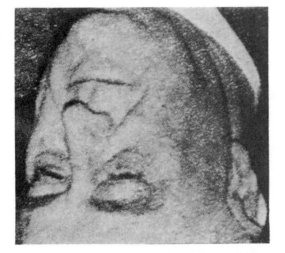

**FIG. 5**

**FIG. 6**

to read, and cursive script almost impossible, when read upside down. Faces look different upside down, and even very familiar ones may be unrecognizable in this orientation.

What distinguishes changes of orientation of this kind from the ones shown in Fig. 1, in such a way that the perceived form itself is affected in the one case but not in others? The difference is that when slant or slope is altered, there is no change in the vertical and horizontal coordinates of the figure and, with respect to these axes, no change in the up–down or left–right "sides" of the figure. When orientation is changed by the rotation shown in Fig. 2, however, such changes are introduced. Assuming for the moment that this way of describing the matter is correct, we may note that there are other ways of rotating a figure, besides the one shown in Fig. 2, that also will result in altering the up–down or left–right directional axes. Thus, if the rotation shown in Fig. 1b is 180°, the figure will end up being inverted without any change in the left–right axis. Or, if the rotation in Fig. 1c is 180°, the figure will end up being reversed from left to right without any change in its up–down axis.

Therefore, perhaps the most general way of referring to all such possible cases is to speak of orientation changes within a frontal plane, that is, changes in which the disoriented figure remains in a plane at right angles to the line of sight (as in Fig. 2), regardless of the way the change of orientation may have been achieved. When a change is achieved by the kind of rotation shown in Fig. 2, I will refer to it as *tilt* or *rotation*; when a figure is turned upside down by the kind suggested in Fig. 1b, I will refer to it as *inversion*; when a figure is reversed by a rotation of the kind suggested in Fig. 1c, I will refer to it as left–right *reversal*. I will refer herein to all changes in a frontal plane as orientation changes, as distinguished from such other types of changes as slope or slant.

The question then arises as to why changes of orientation that affect the directional coordinates of a figure result in alterations of its phenomenal shape, whereas changes of slope or slant, where these axes are not affected, do not. That changes of slant and slope generally do not affect shape, despite the compression of the retinal image, implies some process of correction of the altered image. There is no general agreement about the mechanism underlying such a correction process, but whatever it is, the result is that the compressed axis is psychologically "interpreted" as not compressed. For example, when a circle is seen from a vantage point such as shown in Fig. 1c, with the result that the horizontal axis is compressed and the retinal image is therefore elliptical rather than circular, the process of correction makes the horizontal axis appear as long as the vertical axis. If so, the figure must be a circle and not an ellipse. It is interesting to note that if conditions are such that the observer has not information concerning the slant of the figure in relation to himself, as would be the case in viewing a luminous figure in the dark, he would tend not to correct the compressed image, implicitly "assuming" the figure to be in a frontal plane, and thus would perceive its shape incorrectly.

This last point is a clue concerning the effect of rotation on perceived shape. Normally one would imagine that an observer would assume that the top of a figure is the region he *perceives* to be the top, namely, the region that is uppermost in the scene. If, therefore, a figure is at one time seen in one orientation (for example, Fig. 1a) and another time in another orientation (for example, Fig. 2), and each time the region that is uppermost is perceived as its top, then there is no reason for a process of correction to occur analogous to the one that occurs in the case of altered slant or slope. But, if for any reason, there is some basis for believing a figure is tilted and that therefore some region other than the one uppermost in the scene is its top, then a process of correction may indeed occur. As a matter of fact, this is quite probably what took place for the reader when he viewed Fig. 2, first, because it was stated in the text that this figure was arrived at by rotating Fig. 1a, and second, because the rectangle surrounding the figure in Fig. 1a is seen as tilted in Fig. 2. That this rectangular frame of reference has an effect is evidenced in Fig. 7, which reproduces Fig. 2 exactly but within an untilted rectangle. Certainly a naive observer who views Fig. 7 without any preconceived ideas about orientation will perceive it as quite a different shape from that shown in Fig. 1a.

So it would seem that a major reason why changes of orientation affect phenomenal shape, whereas changes of slant or slope generally do not, is that in the first case there is often no reason to make any correction of the retinal image, while in the second case there is. But there are two qualifications to be made about this conclusion. First, the change induced in perceived shape by compression of the image, even if *not* corrected, is not anywhere near

**FIG. 7**

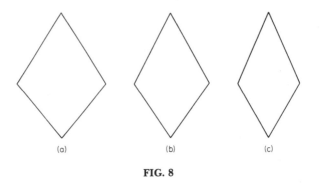

(a)          (b)          (c)

**FIG. 8**

as great as that induced by rotation. As can be seen in Fig. 8, which shows a diamond altered by compression of its horizontal axis, there is still a high degree of similarity between all the variations shown. Second, even where correction is initiated, for example, in the case where the true location of the top, bottom, and sides of a figure are known, often it is still difficult to perceive the figure in the same way as one does when it remains upright. After all, the examples in Figs. 5 and 6 are known to be upside down, but the fact remains they are still hard to make out.

There are, however, a number of other ways in which the retinal image of a figure can be changed, and these have essentially no effect on apparent shape. The location of the image can be changed, and indeed it is constantly undergoing change as we move our eyes from one region of a figure to another. The size of the image also can be changed, and is constantly undergoing such change as a function of changes in our viewing distance. Even with viewing distance held constant and change of image size produced by varia-tions in the physical size of the figure, there still is no effect on phenomenal shape. Gestalt psychologists and others have noted that apparently what matters for shape perception is not the absolute properties of the image—its location or size—but the rela-tionships of parts of the figure to one another. Clearly, in the case of an auditory pattern such as a melody, it is the sequence of *changes* in the pitch of the tones and their rhythmical relationships that are crucial, not the sum of all the specific tones per se. Otherwise, we should not be able to recognize the melody when it is transposed by changing the key. If, therefore, the crucial elements in form perception are the figural *relationships,* why should a change in the figure's overall orientation, which does not alter these relationships, lead to a change in its perceived shape? For example, if a square is "defined" as a four-sided figure with all sides equal in length, with opposite sides parallel, and with four right angles, then these aspects remain unchanged, regardless of the orientation of the figure as a whole. In this regard, it constitutes a real problem why changes of orientation in the frontal plane do lead to changes in phenomenal shape; whereas in the case of changes in slope or slant, modifications do occur in the internal geometry of the image of a figure so that changes in perceived shape are perhaps more to be expected. Yet, in the latter case, they are minimal.

What facts are known about the effect of orientation on phenomenal shape and recognition of shape? Not much more has come out of laboratory studies than can be observed easily in daily life, as illustrated in the various figures shown above. Several studies were undertaken to ascertain the effect of varying *degrees* of change in orientation on the recognizability of forms, and by and large the findings suggest that rotations of 90° have as much of an effect, if not more, than those of 180° (Dearborn, 1899; Gibson & Robinson, 1935; Arnoult, 1954). This is somewhat surprising, because it seems to be the case that materials such as printed or written words and pictures of faces are more difficult to recognize the greater the degree of tilt, as the reader can easily verify for himself.

A good deal of work has also been directed at the question of whether or not young children are adversely affected by orientation of form in the same way adults are. Parents and teachers have noted that children often seem to be unaffected by orientation, to judge by the tendency of preschool children to look at pictures upside down, or in any orientation, without any apparent disturbance and, conversely, by the fact that school-age children have

great difficulty in learning to discriminate letters that are alike
except for orientation (for example, p and d; b and q). Thus it
has been thought that young children, unlike adults, are indifferent
to orientation. However, laboratory studies as yet have failed to
confirm this belief. Certain other experimental findings relating
to the problem of orientation in form perception will be described
in subsequent chapters.

An outline of the main ideas presented in this monograph may
be helpful to the reader.

In Chapter II, evidence will be presented that there are two
distinct factors responsible for the effect of orientation on shape
perception and recognition that heretofore have not been distinguished. One is the effect of perceiving where the top, bottom,
and sides of a figure are as a result of its orientation. If the orientation of a figure is changed, then these directions of the figure
may be perceived differently, and the altered perception leads to
profound phenomenal changes in the figure's shape. Such altered
perception may occur even where there is no change in orientation
at all in the figure's image on the retina. The other factor *is* the
effect of the orientation of the figure's image on the retina. When
the image does not fall in its customary "upright" orientation on
the retina, then, under certain conditions, there is difficulty in perceiving and recognizing the figure.

In Chapter III, an attempt will be made to account for the effect
of a change in the perceived directions of a figure (the first factor
referred to above). It will be argued that the perception of shape
entails an unconscious process of analysis or description of a figure,
and that this includes reference to the directions we call top, bottom,
and sides. Therefore, a figure in one orientation is "described"
quite differently from one in another orientation.

In Chapter IV, an attempt will be made to account for the effect
produced by a change in orientation of the retinal image, the second
factor referred to above (when no change in the perceived directions
of the figure would seem to have occurred). It will be argued that
under these conditions, a process of correction is necessary in order

to "describe" the figure properly. Although information is available as to where the top, bottom, and sides of the figure actually are, these directions are not aligned with the egocentrically given top, bottom, and sides derived from orientational coordinates of the retina. To correct for the misalignment of the two sets of directional coordinates, one must engage in certain cognitive operations similar to those which occur in other cases of perceptual constancy. This process of correction, while generally successful, breaks down under certain conditions and for certain kinds of stimulus material.

In Chapter V, various other theories about the problem will be critically examined, and various implications of the findings will be discussed.

In Chapter VI, implications for a general theory of form perception and recognition are discussed.

Chapter VII is a brief summary.

★
★ ★

CHAPTER II

# Retinal Orientation
# versus Assignment of Directions

When the orientation of a figure is changed, several things are happening simultaneously that must be separated before we can expect to make progress in this area. First, the orientation of the figure's retinal image is changed. Second, the orientation of the figure with respect to gravity and —third—with respect to the visual frame of reference is altered. Which one of these changes causes the change in the figure's phenomenal shape and the consequent failure of recognition? Or do all of them play a role?

It is possible to separate the orientation of the retinal image, which I will herein refer to simply as *retinal orientation*, from the orientation of a figure with respect to gravity or to the visual frame of reference. Ordinarily the latter two factors vary concomitantly, as when a picture on the wall of a room is tilted. Although these can, in turn, be isolated from one another

11

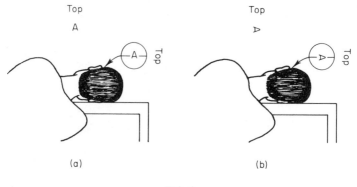

**FIG. 9**

experimentally, I will treat them for the moment as one factor, which I will call *environmental orientation*. One way to isolate retinal orientation from environmental orientation is to require the observer to view a figure when his head is tilted because the eyes tilt with the head.[1] Therefore, if the figure remains environmentally upright, only retinal orientation is changed (Fig. 9a). If the figure is also tilted by the same magnitude as the head, then retinal orientation is not changed, but the perceived environmental orientation of the figure is changed (Fig. 9b). The question at issue is which of these factors is responsible for the altered appearance of disoriented figures? Or are they both implicated?

### Experimental Evidence

Köhler (1940) asked this question and satisfied himself by a simple demonstration that retinal orientation was responsible. He bent down until his head was inverted and looked backwards between

[1] Actually, this is only approximately true. When the head is tilted, the eyes do not remain completely fixed in relation to the head, but turn very slightly back toward the upright (*Augenrollung*, or countertorsion). However, the magnitude of this effect is slight, of the order of about 6° for a 90° head tilt. Therefore, for purposes of the present investigation, a figure that remains upright in the environment gives rise to a retinal image tilted by about the magnitude the head is tilted. Conversely, a figure tilted by the same amount as the head can be considered to be retinally upright.

his legs at a picture of a face held by an assistant. When the picture remained upright, he had difficulty in making it out (retinal disorientation only); when it was held upside down, he had no difficulty (environmental disorientation only). It is easy to verify this observation and, I might add, the same will be found true for printed text and cursive writing. Others have confirmed this finding with a somewhat different technique (see Thouless, 1947; Kanizsa & Tampieri, 1965). Figures such as those shown in Fig. 10 are presented to an observer, who views them with his head inverted. These figures are ambiguous in the sense that in one orientation they represent one face, while turned around they represent

(a)                      (b)                      (c)

**FIG. 10**

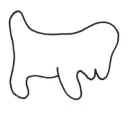 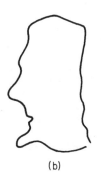

(a)                      (b)

**FIG. 11**

another. The results are quite clear. Observers almost always recognize the face that is retinally upright but environmentally inverted.

Despite this evidence, my own research has led me to believe that more often it is change of environmental orientation that affects phenomenal shape, and that the examples cited above represent special cases. I will therefore come back to these cases and begin with an experiment similar in principle to those described above.

If ambiguous figures are designed such that the tops of the two versions are 90° rather than 180° apart, the outcome is entirely different. The figures shown in Fig. 11 are presented briefly to an observer whose head is tilted 90° (Rock, 1956).[2] If the observer is shown Fig. 11a when his head is tilted 90° counterclockwise, then it is generally seen as a cartoon of a dog rather than a profile of a chef; if Fig. 11b is shown to an observer who is tilted 90° clockwise, it is generally seen as a profile of a bearded man rather than an outline map of the United States. Thus, the environmentally upright rather than the retinally upright version is generally recognized. Stated differently, retinal disorientation does not prevent recognition, but environmental disorientation does. The experiment is predicated on the assumption that the observer will *assume* that whatever is being shown on the screen is upright, that is, the top of the figure is the region uppermost on the screen.

In other experiments novel figures first shown to an upright observer in a training period are presented again in a test period, together with new figures (Rock & Heimer, 1957). In the test, the observer is tilted, and the critical figures each appear twice. These figures either remain environmentally upright or are tilted by the same amount as the observer. They are shown briefly (tachistoscopically) in a series of similar figures, presented one at a time,

---

[2]In all the experiments to be described in this paper, the positioning of the observer was accomplished as follows: for 45° tilts, the head rested against one side of an inverted V-shaped wooden head rest; for 90° tilts, the side of the head rested on a rubber mat on a table; for 180° rotation, the observer stood up, facing away from the figure, bent over and looked backward between his legs; or, he bent over and looked backward with his head along the side of his body.

(a)                                    (b)

**FIG. 12**

and the observer is to say whether or not they are familiar.[3] Figure 12a shows one of the figures in its upright orientation; Fig. 12b shows the figure in its tilted orientation (from Rock, 1956).

The result is that the critical figure that remains environmentally upright is recognized about as frequently as the critical figure in a control experiment where the observer remains upright. In other words, the retinal disorientation in the experimental condition has essentially no adverse effect on recognition. Conversely, the critical figure that remains retinally upright (but is environmentally tilted) is recognized almost as seldom as it is in a control experiment, where the observer is upright and the figure tilted 90°. Thus environmental tilt is about as disturbing as retinal and environmental tilt together.[4]

The same result was obtained in a simple experiment using a square and a diamond figure. In the control condition, observers were shown the square and the diamond separately and asked to describe what they saw. The great majority, of course, described these as a "square" and a "diamond" respectively. In the experimental condition, the observer's head was tilted 45°. Under these conditions, the image of the square is now, retinally speaking, "a diamond," and the image of the diamond is a "square." Nevertheless, the square continued to be described as a square and the diamond continued to be described as a diamond. Hence,

---

[3]Using another technique (Rock, 1956), the two critical test figures for a given training figure are presented briefly in an array of other novel figures of the same style. An example is shown in Fig. 59. The observer must indicate which figure in the array is familiar.

[4]Similar results have been obtained in experiments in which the observer is tilted in the training session and upright in the test session.

it is not retinal orientation but orientation as perceived in the environment that determines phenomenal shape here. An interesting demonstration along these lines is the following: One first forms an afterimage of a square and then tilts his head 45°. The afterimage appears to be a diamond. The same is true if the afterimage is viewed with head tilted but eyes closed. This anticipates a finding to be reported below, namely, that gravitational information alone suffices to determine the environmental orientation that, in turn, is relevant for phenomenal shape.

One characteristic of a square is the impression that it contains right angles, whereas this is not immediately evident in the case of the diamond in Fig. 4. Since Erich Goldmeier (1937) has shown that the spontaneous impression of a right angle depends upon the vertical and horizontal orientation of its sides (see Chapter V, Fig. 61, page 86), the question arises whether this effect depends on the orientation of an angle's sides in the retinal image or in phenomenal space. We have found that viewing the figures in Fig. 61a with head tilted 45° does not eliminate the easy discrimination of the right angle, nor does it bring about such easy discrimination in Fig. 61b.[5] Therefore, the perceived horizontal and vertical directions of the sides of the angle in the environment are what matters. This suggests that the perception of an angle is in part secondary to the perception of the direction of its sides. If we immediately perceive one side as horizontal and the other as vertical, then, *ipso facto*, we "deduce" that the angle enclosed by these sides is 90°. Therefore, perception of a figure as a square or a diamond may be reduced to the perception of the figure's angles, which, in turn, is a function of the perceived environmental directions of its sides.

Further evidence confirming these conclusions comes from a recent experiment on the discrimination of line direction (Attneave & Olson, 1967). It is known that human beings and some animal species find it far easier to discriminate a vertical line from a horizontal line than to discriminate clockwise from counterclockwise

[5] Unpublished research conducted by the author and Robin Leaman.

oblique lines. The investigators raised the question whether this is based on retinal directions or environmental directions, and they tested it by requiring the observer to view these lines with his head tilted 45°. Their measure was the difference in reaction time to either a vertical or horizontal line (the response being a name they first learned to associate with each line) versus reaction time to either oblique line. When the observer was upright, reaction time was significantly shorter to the horizontal or vertical lines than to the obliques, presumably because there was little difficulty in discriminating them from one another. When the observer was tilted, the reaction time to the environmentally vertical and horizontal lines was still shorter than to the oblique lines, despite the fact that the former were then retinally oblique and the latter retinally vertical and horizontal. Attneave and Olson also showed that there was excellent transfer from a session where the observer was upright to one where he was tilted (and vice versa) provided the names given each line in the second session continued to be determined by environmental direction, but that transfer was negative if the names given in the second session were determined on the basis of retinal direction in the two sessions.

All these findings attest to the important effect that the orientation a figure is perceived to have in the environment will have on phenomenal shape. Therefore, one might say that the perception of how things are oriented in the environment logically occurs prior to the perception of shape as a function of orientation. The question then arises as to what factors determine the perception of environmental orientation. But this is a separate topic in the field of perception, and to explore it fully here would take us too far afield. It is sufficient to indicate for now that two factors, essentially, determine how we perceive things to be oriented in the world: gravity and the visual frame of reference. That gravity alone is such a determinant is evidenced by the fact that one can judge in a totally dark field which directions are vertical and which are horizontal when viewing luminous lines, even when one's own body is tilted. That the visual frame of reference is a determinant is shown by the strong effect exerted on these perceived directions when the object being judged is embedded in a physically tilted room. So in what follows, it will simply be assumed that either of these factors—and of course, both together—influence our perception of how things are oriented in the world.

Another problem is whether each of these factors alone, in affecting perceived figural orientation, will also influence phenomenal shape. In one of our experiments, the observer viewed figures through a circular opening with his head tilted 90°. The procedure was essentially like the technique described earlier (see footnote 3, page 15) in which the two critical figures were presented along with other alternatives in an array, and the observer was to select the familiar one. One critical figure appeared upright in the environment, and the other was tilted 90° so as to be retinally upright. Nothing was visible except the circular array of figures, so that no visual reference lines served to indicate the vertical and horizontal axes of space. Therefore, it can be assumed that only gravity was determining environmental direction.[6] The results were comparable to the condition described earlier, namely, that the environmentally upright figure was selected most of the time.

The influence of the visual frame of reference was demonstrated in experiments in which an upright observer, looking through a prism, viewed a room within which could be seen the array of figures. The prism had the effect of disorienting the retinal image so that the room appeared tilted. The critical figures in the array were presented in such a way that, through the prism, one gave rise to an upright retinal image (but appeared environmentally tilted). The other gave rise to a tilted image that was upright with

---

[6]Proof that this was the case came somewhat unexpectedly when it was discovered that a direction not vertical in space but one tilted 10–20° appeared vertical to our observers. Clearly we had run into the Aubert effect, according to which a constant error occurs in setting a luminous rod in the dark to the vertical when the observer judges from a quite tilted position (see Aubert, 1861). This was therefore taken into account by aligning one critical figure with the direction that prior testing had indicated appeared vertical in space to that observer. The other critical figure was tilted 90° so as to be retinally upright for the observer.

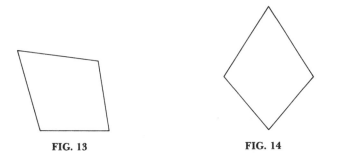

FIG. 13                                       FIG. 14

respect to the walls and other verticals within the room and, therefore, appeared upright in that sense. The result, again, was that
the retinally tilted but phenomenally upright figure was selected
more frequently. An effect of the visual frame of reference was
mentioned in Chapter I. Compare Figs. 2 and 7 (pages 2 and 5)
with Fig. 1a (page 2).

## Symmetry

A figure can be symmetrical about some axis, as is the case in
Fig. 13, but the symmetry is often not perceived. It is perceived
in Fig. 14, which is Fig. 13 tilted clockwise by about 45°. Ernst
Mach had noted that it is primarily symmetry about the vertical
axis that causes a figure to be perceived as symmetrical, and the
contrast between Figs. 13 and 14 bears this out (Mach, 1914).[7]
One explanation for the fact that phenomenal symmetry requires
a vertical axis of symmetry involves the orientation of the image
on the retina and, consequently, the orientation of the projection
of this image to the visual cortex. Perhaps, as Mach thought, it
has something to do with the bilateral symmetry of the motor
apparatus of the eyes or with the bilateral symmetry of the brain.
We therefore conducted a study to find out if this important
feature of phenomenal shape depends on whether the axis of symmetry is vertical in the retinal image or whether it is perceived

[7]This fact was also demonstrated experimentally by Goldmeier (1937).

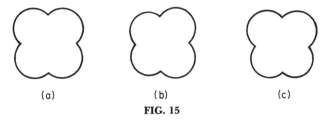

(a)                    (b)                    (c)

**FIG. 15**

as vertical (Rock & Leaman, 1963). We used a figure such as the one shown above in Fig. 15a as a standard (symmetrical about horizontal and vertical axes), and asked our subjects to indicate which figure, 15b or 15c, appeared to be more like Fig. 15a. Figure 15b was altered so as to eliminate symmetry about the vertical axis but to preserve it about the horizontal axis; in Fig. 15c, the converse was true.

When the observer was upright, Fig. 15c was generally selected, presumably because it preserved an impression of symmetry, whereas Fig. 15b did not. Now, when the observer was tilted 45°, he still selected Fig. 15c as more like Fig. 15a than 15b, despite the fact that in this situation neither figure preserved vertical symmetry in the retinal image. In fact, the effect was about as strong as when the observer was upright. Hence, phenomenal symmetry that had been known to depend upon the orientation of the axis of symmetry is now seen to depend upon the perceived environmental direction of that axis, not the orientation of the retinal image of that axis. Conversely, if the three figures are tilted 45° as shown in Fig. 16, there is no favoring of Fig. 16c over 16b when the observer is upright, as is to be expected. But there is also no favoring of Fig. 16c when the observer is tilted 45°, although, in this case the latter figure is symmetrical about the vertical retinal axis.

Therefore, it seems quite clear that if a figure is symmetrical about an axis that, for whatever reason, we perceive to be vertical, it will appear to be symmetrical; otherwise it will not. This suggests that we pay particular attention to how the left and right sides of a figure compare to one another. If they are the same, we note that they are, and the result is an impression of symmetry; if they

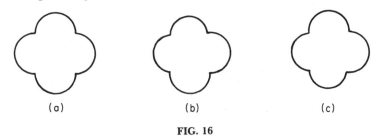

(a)          (b)          (c)

**FIG. 16**

differ, we note the difference, and the result is an impression of asymmetry.

## The Assignment of Directions

One can interpret the findings described above to mean that gravitational or visual information can affect phenomenal shape, and let it go at that. Or one can argue, as I do, that what matters as far as orientation is concerned in form perception is which part of a figure is designated as top, which as bottom, and so forth. Regardless of which source of information is available, a certain direction within a figure will be seen as vertical, and the phenomenally uppermost end of that direction will therefore delineate the top of the figure. It seems natural that an observer should assign directions to a figure on the basis of how it appears to be oriented in the environment, provided that the figure is in an environmentally vertical plane. What is uppermost in a picture on a wall normally *is* the top. It would be surprising, and rather egocentric, if a tilted observer were to assign direction on the basis of projecting his own bodily coordinates onto the figure.

The correctness of this interpretation is borne out by the finding that there is another source of information for figural directions. When this is set into conflict with retinal orientation per se, it too wins out, just as environmental orientation does in the experiments already described. One can simply tell an observer where the top of a figure is or where it will appear (in the case of a brief exposure), and this serves as directional information. Thus, if the reader chooses to perceive the diamond in Fig. 4 (Chapter I, page 2) as a tilted square, which means he now sees one of the upper *sides* rather than the uppermost corner as "top," then the figure will look like a square. For this reason, sophisticated observers are poor subjects for work on this problem. They may decide to consider a region as "top" when the purpose of the experiment is that they do not do so.

As evidence on this point, consider the following variations in the experiments on symmetry described above. If an upright observer is told that the figures in Fig. 15 are tilted 45° clockwise, Fig. 15c is no longer selected more frequently than Fig. 15b. We have destroyed the perceived symmetry about the vertical axis (present *both* retinally and environmentally) by the expedient of instructing the observer where the top of the figure is. Conversely, if upright observers are told that the figures in Fig. 16 are tilted 45° clockwise, then Fig. 16c again is favored strongly over **Fig.** 16b, presumably because we have reestablished its vertical symmetry by the simple expedient of informing the observer about the location of the vertical axis. In the original experiment with *this* figure, there was no preference for Fig. 16c over 16b. Note that in this condition, neither retinal nor environmental vertical coordinates create symmetry in the figure. The information supplied and the set it engenders must overcome the absence of symmetry based on those determinants, and yet, it does so (Rock & Leaman, 1963).[8] Other research (some of which will be described later) and simple demonstrations have repeatedly confirmed that information, set, or intention can lead to perceiving a figure in a given orientation, and that this step in turn leads to major changes in phenomenal shape.

---

[8] This kind of effect has been confirmed by Attneave and Reid (1968), who followed up the previous study of Attneave and Olson (1967) by instructing subjects to think of the top of their head as "up" when their head was tilted. They found that for such subjects, objectively oblique lines now tended to be discriminated more rapidly from one another than were objectively horizontal and vertical lines, and transfer from one session to another was a function of the phenomenal orientation of the lines as determined by these instructions or by other information rather than by retinal orientation.

## Conclusions

All these lines of evidence lead to the conclusion that there are to this as the assignment of direction factor. I think it safe to ception when a figure's orientation is changed. One is the effect of the subjective assignment of directions to a figure. I will refer to this as the assignment of directions factor. I think it safe to assert that any figure other than a circle will look different, often completely different, if the assignment of directions is changed.[9] This is true even if there is no change in retinal orientation. It must be borne in mind, however, that if a figure is quite familiar, it may be virtually impossible to create such a condition. Thus, faces, letters, text, and the like usually carry their own directions with them, regardless of their physical orientation.[10]

The other factor is the effect of a change in retinal orientation, and I will refer to it as the retinal factor. Here it would seem that the problem is not one of incorrect assignment of directions, because the effect has been observed primarily with precisely that type of material that, I have just argued, carries correct directionalization. Furthermore, the effect is best isolated under conditions where the figure remains upright in the environment (so that it is clear to the observer where the top and bottom of the figure are located) and is viewed from a tilted or inverted position. As noted, printed words, cursive writing, and faces clearly undergo some change in recognizability when retinal disorientation alone is imposed.

[9]This is not to deny that a circle, too, has a phenomenal top, bottom, and sides, but only to point out that a shift in the assignment of such directions in the case of a circle will not result in any change in its perceived shape.

[10]This is one reason why Köhler (1940) failed to find any effect other than one based on retinal orientation. He used a figure of a face. When it was inverted in the environment, the observer realized this. Of course, under conditions where there is no set for a very familiar object, it is undoubtedly possible to bring about an incorrect assignment of directions in certain cases and thus to bring about failure of recognition. Thus, for example, if ◖ is presented in a series of geometric shapes, it will certainly not be seen as a tilted D, perhaps even if the observer's head is tilted 90° counterclockwise so that the image is retinally upright.

Having established that altered orientation has two apparently distinct effects on form perception, I will now attempt to clarify the nature of each separately.

★

★  ★

# CHAPTER III

# The Assignment
# of Direction Factor

Why should a change in the subjective assignment of directions to a figure alter its phenomenal shape? It is plausible to think that the essence of shape is given by the internal geometry of a figure. Thus, a square is different from a triangle because it has four equal sides, its opposite sides are parallel, and its corners are right angles, whereas a triangle has three straight sides and three corners, etc. These features do not change at all as a function of figural orientation; at least, objectively they do not change. Phenomenally, however, these features often *do* change. The angles in the diamond (Fig. 4, Chapter I, page 2) do not look like right angles, whereas right-angle corners are central in one's perception of the square.

Therefore, a phenomenal square is not merely an equilateral quadrilateral having parallel sides. It is that and more—namely, a figure so oriented that its sides are perceived as horizontal and vertical and its angles as right angles. The only explanation I have been able to provide as to why orientation has this effect on shape is rather simple. An object looks different in different orientations because part of our cognition takes into account its directions in the environment. Consider Fig. 13 (Chapter II, page 19). Phenomenally, it appears as an irregular quadrilateral resting solidly on a base and skewed to one side on top. If we were to describe it, this is approximately what we might say. Consider Fig. 14 next (Chapter II, page 19). It appears as a symmetrical, diamond-shaped figure balanced on a point, and this is how we would describe *it*. Yet Fig. 14 is Fig. 13 tilted clockwise by about 45°. It seems that the perception of shape must, therefore, entail a process of cognitive description or analysis that takes into account external figural relationships as well as internal ones, the external ones being those that relate the figure to the up–down, left–right directions assigned to it. Such a process of description is not consciously represented, and it can hardly be verbal in nature. Verbal description simply could not do justice to any but the most elementary nuances of a figure. Furthermore, form perception is surely present in animals and preverbal infants.

### The Effect of Degree of Orientation Change on Shape

What implications can be drawn from this analysis about the probable effect of varying degrees of disorientation on phenomenal shape? As noted earlier, investigations thus far have not revealed any lawful relationship, except for the finding that change of orientation does impair recognizability. On the other hand, we do know from informal observation that material such as words or faces seems to be more difficult to make out when turned upside down than when rotated only through a lesser angle. Now that we have distinguished two separate factors, however, the possibility arises that the previous failure to confirm this observation is the result of confounding the two. In fact, it is a good guess that the essentially progressive deterioration in recognition of word figures and the like with increasing degrees of tilt is based exclusively on the retinal factor. (This matter will be discussed further in the next chapter.)

As far as the assignment of direction factor is concerned, there is already good reason for predicting that the function relating degree of tilt to degree of phenomenal change will be unique (or at least different) for each figure. For example, it is perfectly obvious that the maximum change for a square would necessarily occur at 45°; for an equilateral triangle it would occur at 60°; the maximum change for a vertically symmetrical figure most probably would occur at 45 or 90° because at 180° the same axis of the figure will be vertical again.

With these considerations in mind, we conducted a study of the effect of varying degrees of tilt on recognition of novel figures (Olshansky, 1966).[1] The general plan entailed exposure of a given figure in a certain orientation during the training period and presentation of that same figure in a different orientation in the test period. In the test, the observer was to indicate if a figure was one of those shown before. In order not to introduce any change in retinal orientation from training to test, however, the orientation of the figure with respect to the observer was the same in both training and test. In other words, to ensure that there would be no change in retinal orientation, whatever was done by way of changing a figure's orientation was also done with respect to the observer's orientation. Figure 17 illustrates the procedure schematically, with letters substituted for novel figures.

For a given figure (for example, A in Fig. 17) the observer was tilted by a certain angle in training, and the figure was also tilted by the same angle from a base-line position that was (sometimes arbitrarily) taken to be its upright orientation. In the test, the observer was always upright, and the figure was presented in its upright orientation. The same observer would also be shown other figures in training (for example, B or C in Fig. 17) which he would look at

---

[1]Since this study has not been published previously, further details of the procedure and results are given in the Appendix (pages 131–139).

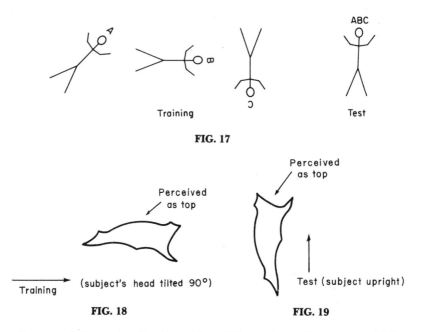

Training                          Test

**FIG. 17**

**FIG. 18**          **FIG. 19**

from a differently tilted position. Then these figures would be shown upright in the test, with the observer also upright.

We assumed that the observer would consider the top of a figure to be the region that was uppermost in the environment. In fact, several steps were taken, including instructions to this effect, to ensure that he would do so. This being the case, the following situation prevails for any given figure. When seen in training, a particular region is perceived to be the top (and consistent with this, other regions are perceived to be the bottom, left, and right sides). For example, consider the case where Fig. 18 is tilted 90° clockwise from its base-line orientation and is seen by an observer who in training is also tilted 90° clockwise. The region toward the top of the page is perceived as its top. In the test, however with the observer and figure now upright, the upper part of Fig. 19 is perceived to be the top. Therefore, for this figure, there is a change in perceived figural orientation of 90° from training to

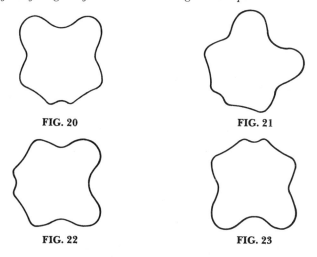

FIG. 20

FIG. 21

FIG. 22

FIG. 23

test. *But*, there is no change in its retinal orientation, because the figure's image is in the same orientation in both training and test. For other observers who saw this figure, there was a *different* magnitude of *change* of orientation from training to test, but in every case the figure's orientation and the observer's orientation were always linked together, so that there was never any change of retinal orientation from training to test. The orientation changes examined in this experiment were 0, 45, 90, and 180°, inversion, and left–right reversal.

As expected, the outcome for each figure was different from that of other figures, although there were certain general trends. For example, wherever the change of orientation of a figure was such that it appeared symmetrical in training but not in the test, or conversely, appeared asymmetrical in training and symmetrical in the test, there was a marked decrease in recognition. To illustrate this, consider Fig. 20. This is the way it was oriented in the test for all observers, and it appears symmetrical. Only 53% of the observers who had seen this figure in training in the 45° tilted orientation shown in Fig. 21 recognized it in the test. Only 62% of those who had seen it in training in the 90° tilted orientation

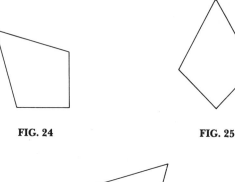

**FIG. 24**                          **FIG. 25**

**FIG. 26**

shown in Fig. 22 recognized it. In neither of these training orientations does it appear symmetrical. Yet for a group that remained
upright in training and test, and therefore, saw it in the *same* orientation in training and test, recognition was 86%. Also, recognition
was high for observers who saw this figure so oriented in training
that phenomenal symmetry was preserved, as in Fig. 23. Here the
figure is rotated 180°, but recognition on the test was as high as
in the control condition.

Figure 24 provides an example of the test orientation of a figure
that does not appear symmetrical. Although a group that saw this
figure in the same orientation in training and test recognized it
91% of the time, observers who saw it in the 45° tilted position
shown in Fig. 25 only recognized it 28% of the time. In this orientation it *does* appear symmetrical. Recognition was much higher for
observers who saw this figure in training in an orientation that
did not produce a symmetrical appearance (as it did not have in
the test). This is exemplified in the left–right reversal shown in
Fig. 26.[2] Here recognition was 76%.

[2]In the case of left–right reversals, the observer was upright in training and
test, and only the orientation of the figure was changed.

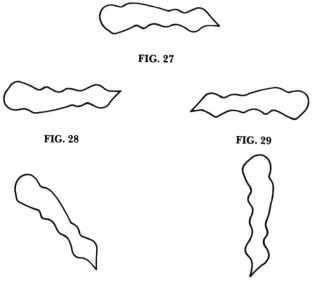

FIG. 27

FIG. 28          FIG. 29

FIG. 30          FIG. 31

Another general trend is related to the orientation of the long axis of the figure. Consider a figure such as that shown in Fig. 27. Its long axis is horizontal. Changes in orientation that kept the long axis horizontal tended to be far less detrimental to recognition than those which altered that orientation. Subjects who saw this figure in the same orientation in training and test recognized it 81% of the time. Those who saw it inverted (Fig. 28) or left–right reversed (Fig. 29) in training recognized it 86 and 67% of the time, respectively. But those who saw it tilted 45° (Fig. 30) or 90° (Fig. 31) recognized it only 43 and 28% of the time, respectively.

Another example is shown in Fig. 32, where the condition of

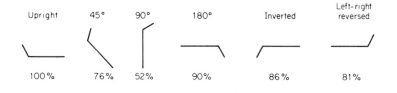

FIG. 32

training is labeled at the top and the percentage of recognition is given at the bottom of each figure. The figure in the upright orientation is seen in the test by observers in all conditions.

It is noteworthy that in many of these examples—and they are typical—changes of 45 or 90° proved to be much more detrimental to recognition than those of 180° rotation, inversion, or left–right reversal. There would seem to be two reasons as to why this is the case. Rotation of 180°, inversion, or left–right reversal will not produce a change in the perception of symmetry or asymmetry. If a figure appears to be symmetrical in training, it will remain so in the test; if it appears to be asymmetrical in training, it will remain so in the test. In the case of all other angular changes, however, a change in symmetry or asymmetry may occur. This is because phenomenal symmetry or asymmetry is a function of the vertical axis, and the orientation of the axis does not change in 180° rotation, inversion, or left–reversal. It is also true that 180° rotation, inversion, or reversal will not produce a change in the long axis of a figure. All other changes of orientation will alter it.

Although the changes that occur for a given degree of orientation change are clearly a function of the characteristics of a specific figure, it may be of some interest to consider the combined results of all figures. The percentage of correct recognitions of all 14 figures used in this experiment for all conditions of orientation change are given in Table 1.

**TABLE 1**
RECOGNITION OF TEST FIGURES[a]

|  | Change of orientation from training to test | | | | | |
|---|---|---|---|---|---|---|
|  | Upright | 45° | 90° | 180° | Inversion | Left–right reversal |
| Correct (%) | 86 | 58 | 60 | 74 | 68 | 79 |
| S.D. | 1.5 | 3.3 | 4.1 | 3.2 | 3.1 | 1.7 |

[a]Each entry is based on 14 figures, each of which was seen by 21 subjects.

It can be seen that of all conditions of orientation change, the left–right reversal condition has the least detrimental effect on recognition. This is what one would expect, because the phenomenal characteristics of a figure are essentially unchanged when it is rotated into the mirror image of itself. That is to say, whether a figure is symmetrical or not, whether it is elongated in one direction or not, whether it rests upon a stable base or not, and so forth is not changed by a left–right reversal. Up and down are very different directions phenomenally, but left and right are more or less equivalent directions in the sense that they both refer to the sides of a figure. The reason why symmetry is only perceived when the axis of symmetry is vertical is probably that the identical halves of the figure then fall in equivalent phenomenal directions. The fact already mentioned that children (and even adults) and animals have difficulty distinguishing left from right, and the related fact that young children and animals find it exceedingly difficult, if not impossible, to discriminate mirror-image figures from their obverse counterparts but do not find it difficult to discriminate inverted figures from their upright counterparts is all part of this fundamental equivalence of the left and right sides.

There is not very much difference between the effect of 180° rotation and inversion. Both entail inversion of the figure from training to test and, hence, the only difference between the two is in the left–right orientation of the figure. One might be inclined to predict that inversion would lead to less change than 180° rotation because the left side of the figure remains on the left and the right side remains on the right. However, each side is upside down, so that there may remain little that is phenomenally similar. Furthermore, a left–right exchange of sides itself does not introduce much change in the appearance of a figure, as witness the results of the left–right reversal condition.

Perhaps the most interesting aspect of the overall trend is the fact that while 180° rotation and inversion changes do lead to an appreciable decline in recognition, the 45 and 90° changes lead

to a much greater decline. Some reasons for this have been suggested above. If one ignores the observations in daily life that
suggest a maximum disturbance at 180° rotation (and which
will be analyzed further in the next chapter), this trend does
not do violence to any a priori considerations. It is interesting
to note that a transformation of 45°, which yields only a slight
effect for retinal change, yields a maximum effect for change
of assigned directions.

## The Perception of Tactually Disoriented Figures

If the analysis about figural orientation offered in this chapter
is correct—that a change in assignment of directions leads to
an altered "description" of the figure—then such effects ought
not to be restricted to visual perception. Suppose one were to
experience by touch alone a familiar shape that was tilted from
its customary orientation. If one did not know that the figure
was tilted, the altered assignment of directions ought to so affect its phenomenal shape that it would not be recognizable.

We have recently demonstrated this fact.[3] In one experiment,
analogous to those described earlier on visual perception, the
observer first felt with his fingers three different forms cut out
of plastic (see Fig. 33). These were mounted on a horizontal stem
in such a way that they remained in a fixed orientation but could
nevertheless be easily examined with the fingers. The observer
could not see the figures, and was told he would be given a
recognition test shortly. Then these figures were randomly
arranged with four others in a test series of seven figures. The
observer explored each manually and was asked to say if he
recognized any of these from the training period. For different
groups of observers, one of the three figures experienced in
training was now tilted 90°, but no reference to orientation was
made by the experimenter.

[3]The experiments were performed by Ben Susswein.

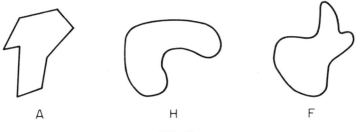

A H F

**FIG. 33**

**TABLE 2**

TACTUAL RECOGNITION OF UPRIGHT AND TILTED FIGURES

| Figure | Number of times presented upright | Number correct | (%) | Number of times presented tilted | Number correct | (%) |
|--------|------|------|--------|------|------|--------|
| A | 40 | 25 | (62.5) | 15 | 5 | (33.3) |
| H | 40 | 22 | (55) | 15 | 6 | (40) |
| F | 40 | 26 | (65) | 15 | 5 | (33.3) |
| Total: | 120 | 73 | (61) | 45 | 16 | (35.5) |

The results are presented in Table 2 in terms of the percentage of recognition of each figure when presented upright or tilted in the test. There were only a negligible number of false recognitions of the noncritical test figures. It is clear that tactual recognition fell off appreciably when the figures were tilted in the test.

A similar result was obtained in another experiment when very familiar shapes were tested. In this case a training period was not required. The observer was told that he would feel some figures with his fingers that he would not be able to see, and that he was to indicate if he recognized any as familiar. He was then presented with a series of seven figures, among which were three of the following four familiar objects: a car, a ship, a boot, or a bell. For any one observer, one of the three was tilted 90°. The other four figures were various shapes. As can be seen in Table 3, recognition was much poorer when the familiar shapes were tilted.

**TABLE 3**
TACTUAL RECOGNITION OF FAMILIAR SHAPES

| Figure | Number of times presented upright | Number correct | (%) | Number of times presented tilted | Number correct | (%) |
|--------|-----------------------------------|----------------|-----|-----------------------------------|----------------|-----|
| Car | 20 | 12 | (60) | 10 | 3 | (30) |
| Ship | 20 | 13 | (65) | 10 | 3 | (30) |
| Boot | 40 | 13 | (32) | 20 | 1 | (5) |
| Bell | 20 | 6 | (30) | 10 | 3 | (30) |
| Total: | 100 | 44 | (44) | 50 | 10 | (20) |

Thus, it seems evident that the effect of disorientation on phenomenal shape is not a uniquely visual phenomenon. These findings also can be viewed as additional evidence that it is not the change of orientation in the retinal image which typically affects the phenomenal shape of visually disoriented figures, since similar effects are obtained in another sense modality. Nor is it likely that the altered perception of tactually disoriented figures results from a change in the specific muscular sensations experienced during training and test, because it is unlikely that the observer repeats the same movements in exploring the object in the test. Furthermore, in the experiment on familiar shapes, there was no prior tactual exploration of the object, at least of a kind that would be at all comparable to that of the test. Therefore it seems likely that this effect is caused by incorrect assignment of directions, leading to changes in perceived shape.

## Why Does Recognition Occur at All
## When Directions Are Incorrectly Assigned?

One might well ask the question why recognition ever occurs when a change of orientation results in altered assignment of directions to a figure. After all, the phenomenal difference

**FIG. 34**

between two orientations of a physically identical figure is often as great or greater than that between two physically different figures. For example, Fig. 34 is far from congruent with Fig. 13, but looks very similar to it; whereas Fig. 14, which is physically identical with Fig. 13, looks totally different (to a naïve observer, of course).

There are several possible answers to this question. First, many of the figures we included were of a distinct type or had a certain unique style. For example, the figure shown in Fig. 32 was one of two open-line figures used and was very different from the other open-line figure. Hence, regardless of orientation, an observer in the test might have noted that he had been looking at the same kind of line figure he had seen before. (This, in turn, might have led him to realize it was, in fact, the same figure in a new orientation.)[4]

Second, the observer did not always assign the direction "top" to the region of the figure which was uppermost in the environment, as it was intended he should. If he did not, for whatever reason, then there may have been no change in such assigned direction from training to test, as intended. In that case, of course, there is no reason for recognition to fail. (See a discussion of this problem on page 138 of the Appendix.)

---

[4]We could have eliminated recognition on this basis had we included many buffer figures in the test for each type of training figure, but we chose not to do so because of other considerations. Because we did not include such items, we cannot determine the number of observers who said "yes" regardless of what figure was shown in the test. Thus, if a good deal of guessing took place, as many as 50% of the "yes" responses per figure could represent the chance base line. If so, the result of 58% for the 45° condition signifies little genuine recognition.

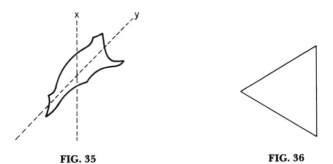

FIG. 35                              FIG. 36

One reason why this might happen is that some figures have axes of orientation of their own, so to speak—an intrinsic orientation. A given direction may have been seen to be the vertical axis of a figure regardless of its spatial orientation or of instructions or set to assign directions differently. For example, in Fig. 35 it may be difficult to see the direction indicated by the line $x$ as the vertical axis; rather the direction indicated by the line $y$ seems to be the natural vertical axis. Therefore, when seen in training in the orientation shown, the directional assignment might have been identical with that made during the test in which the figure was in an upright orientation (see the Appendix, Fig. 69, Item 4b). An equilateral triangle shown oriented as in Fig. 36 cannot be perceived as a figure with its vertical axis determined by the vertical of the page. Rather, its vertical axis will be perceived as bisecting one of its apices, and that apex will then be perceived as top (Attneave, 1968).[5] It has also been demonstrated that children have preferences for certain orientations of novel figures as right side up, preferring the focal part of the figure to be at the top (Ghent, 1960, 1961, 1964). Therefore, if this part is at the bottom of the figure, they may consider it to be upside down.

[5]Such a triangle is an ambiguous figure in the sense that the top may suddenly shift to one of the other apices. In each case, it looks different (that is, it looks like a differently oriented triangle) because phenomenal symmetry emerges about the axis momentarily perceived as vertical, thus rendering the figure phenomenally isosceles. Apparently the figure can have only one phenomenal axis of symmetry at a time.

Apart from the reasons already given, it is undoubtedly the case that occasionally a figure is recognized despite the fact there is a change in the way directions are assigned to it. Such recognition may occur because the change in assignment of directions does not lead to a major change in phenomenal shape. A left–right reversal would be a change of this kind, and a 180° rotation or inversion may be a change of this kind for some figures for the reasons outlined earlier. In these cases, recognition may occur without the observer realizing that there is any change in the figure's orientation. It simply looks much the same in its new orientation.

However, in some cases, recognition of disoriented figures seems to be based on an awareness of the new orientation. But how is it possible to know that a figure is tilted or upside down if, as I have argued, its shape is influenced so strongly by the orientation? Of course, if for any reason (such as any of the reasons suggested above—for example, that the figure has its own intrinsic axis of orientation), the observer assigns directions to a figure in the test in the same way he did in training, he will recognize the figure because there is no change in its subjectively assigned directions, even when it is tilted. The figure will be recognized and perceived as tilted from an upright environmental orientation.[6]

But suppose we are not dealing with cases of this kind, but rather with cases where the directions assigned to a test figure *are* changed. Undoubtedly, some of the time such a figure will be recognized, and the fact that it is in a new orientation will also be perceived. Only two explanations seem possible:

[6]I stated earlier that often a figure—such as a face—will *not* suffer from an incorrect assignment of directions when disoriented because it is immediately apparent that it is disoriented. But must it not first be recognized before it can be evident that it is such-and-such figure in a new orientation? And how can it be recognized first if the new orientation alters its appearance? One answer that suggests itself is that a figure may have sufficiently distinctive internal features—such as eyes in a face or a string of letterlike characters as in a printed word—and these will form the basis of recognition of the kind of object it is, which, in turn, will lead to awareness that the figure is disoriented with respect to the environmental up–down axis.

1. The purely internal figural relationships retain their psychological identity, and they are not wholly incorporated into the cognition that takes account of their orientation. This forms the basis of recognition, since the internal figural relationships are unchanged.

2. The assigning of directions to a figure is not always as permanent and unvarying as one might think. There is instead a certain amount of mental trial and error, or shifting, in which now one part of a figure and now another is tried as the top, and so forth. When the correct part is momentarily made the top, the figure is recognized and so is its tilt.[7] Whereas this explanation may seem far fetched at the moment, it is in keeping with certain speculations about perpetual organization of other kinds (Epstein & De Shazo, 1961).

The evidence derived from experiments with various species of animals by and large suggests that a figure is perceived as different when it is encountered in a new orientation. In other words, a figure in a new orientation does not seem to be recognized. If it were, there would be great difficulty in learning to discriminate figures that differ from one another merely by orientational transformations—much more so than in learning to discriminate figures that actually are different from one another, which is generally not the case. Also, there is generally little transfer of a learned discrimination when the positive figure is presented upside down (Zusne, 1970, Chapter 8).[8] This attests to the fundamental nature of the role of direction in form perception. The physical identity of the upright and inverted figure does not lead to phenomenal identity or even similarity. (The exception to this rule is the case of left–right (or mirror) reversal,

[7]When the subject is tilted, as in the training condition of the Olshansky (1966) experiment, there may be a tendency to shift the directions assigned so as to be congruent with his egocentric up–down, left–right directions.

[8]Of course, there are important species differences concerning reaction to orientation of form, and it is possible that entirely different mechanisms are responsible for these reactions. The results of experiments also differ as a function of type of figure tested, type or degree of orientation change, and so forth.

where there is great difficulty in learning to discriminate. But this is what we would expect if such transformations looked as alike to animals as they do to human beings.) Presumably animals would not be capable of shifting, nor would they tend to shift, figural directions from those indicated by gravity and visual information.

Thus, the answer to the question raised in this section, namely, why does recognition occur when directions are presumably incorrectly assigned to a figure, would be as follows:

1. The figure is still similar "stylistically," despite its new orientation.

2. The kind of change in assignment of directions is not one that drastically alters shape (for example, left–right reversal).

3. For one reason or another, the observer achieves the correct assignment of direction. He may do so deliberately (see the Appendix, page 138), or because the figure has its own intrinsic directions, or because details of the figure lead to recognition of the object and its tilted orientation, or because he unconsciously rotates the directional coordinates (or the figure) in his imagination until the correct orientation occurs.

4. If none of these is true, then it would have to be argued that the internal geometry of the figure to some extent retains its psychological identity despite the changed assignment of directions, and that this forms the basis for recognition.

★

★  ★

CHAPTER IV

# The Retinal Factor

The evidence presented in the last two chapters makes it clear beyond any doubt that a change in the subjective assignment of directions will result in a change in the phenomenal shape of a figure. The altered directions lead to a different cognition of the figure. This can be considered the explanation of the problem we started with, namely, the effect of change in figural orientation on perceived form and form recognition. However, this explanation does not seem to cover the cases where there is no change in assigned directions, as when upright figures such as faces or words are viewed by a tilted observer. Yet the difficulty in recognition of such material under these conditions is striking. Here the cause of the difficulty in recognition would seem to be a direct function of the change in retinal orientation, rather than a function of change in assigned direction. There are, therefore, two new problems to be faced. One is to discover the conditions under which difficulty in recognition as a result of retinal change occurs, including the essential nature of the material that *is* subject to this effect. This problem arises because we have seen that under many conditions and with a variety of figures, retinal change per se appears to have *no* effect. The other problem is to understand *why,* under certain conditions and for certain material, there is an effect of retinal change, although there is no change in the directions assigned to the figure. The latter problem will be considered first.

### The Basis of Perceptual Change
### with Change of Retinal Orientation

When a figure appears to have the same shape and, therefore, is recognized despite the altered orientation of its retinal image—as in most of our experiments—this outcome can be considered an achievement analogous to a perceptual constancy. The retinal image and, therefore, its cortical representation, is drastically altered, but by taking into account additional information concerning orientation, a constancy of shape is achieved.[1]

It must be assumed that the specific orientation of the image is first perceived or at least discriminated by the perceptual system. The basis for this claim can be made clear by analogy to the problem of perception of the vertical direction from a tilted position of the observer's body in a dark field. Obviously the true orientation in the environment of a luminous line can be only "deduced" by the perceptual system if (1) the physical orientation of the image on the retina is discriminated, and (2) information concerning the physical orientation of the observer himself is available. In the same way, a shape can be correctly apprehended only if (1) the orientation of its retinal image is detected and (2) informa-

[1]This is not to be confused with shape constancy—the constancy of perceived shape despite the slant or slope of the plane of the figure with respect to the observer.

tion is available concerning the way the figure is oriented—for example, the kind of information that can be derived from the physical orientation of the observer.

In the case of perceptual constancies such as size and shape, there is some disagreement about the question of whether or not there is any *perception* of the physical properties of the proximal stimulus—for example, visual angle in size perception. I am of the opinion that we can perceive the difference in extensity (or size of field subtended) between a near and far stimulus even while perceiving its objective size as constant (Rock & McDermott, 1964). I believe we also perceive the shape based on the retinal image of an object at a slant, even while taking slant into account and perceiving the objective shape veridically. Thus when viewing a circle at a slant, we see both an "ellipse" and a circle. Of course, the perception of objective size and shape is dominant. In the same way, we can be aware of the orientation of the retinal image even while we are veridically perceiving the spatial orientation of the object, based on taking into account the position of one's body. This awareness is phenomenally experienced as egocentric orientation.

Retinal orientation and perceived egocentric orientation are essentially linked, the latter being a function of the former. In other words, the way an object is perceived to be oriented in relation to the self seems to depend on how its image is oriented. To isolate this aspect of perceived orientation from the perceived orientation of an object in the environment, the ideal procedure is to rotate an object about a vertical axis in a horizontal plane. In one such experiment, illustrated in Fig. 37, the observer lies in a supine position in a dark room and views a horizontal luminous rod above him, which is pivoted about a vertical axis (Rock, 1954, 1966). Changes in orientation of the rod are thus only egocentric, since in all its positions it is orthogonal to the direction of gravity. It was demonstrated that the rod appears to be parallel to the long axis of the body (or just to the sagittal plane of the head) when its image falls in approximately the

Luminous
rod

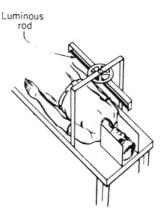

**FIG. 37**

vertical retinal orientation. Similarly, the egocentric "horizontal" is a function of essentially horizontal orientation of the image.

The same relations hold in the more complicated situation where the object judged also changes orientation with respect to the vertical and horizontal directions of the environment. For example, if the observer is tilted in the environment, the line must be tilted by the same magnitude—so that its image remains retinally vertical—in order that it may continue to appear egocentrically "vertical." It will then, of course, appear tilted in the environment, but if instructed properly, the observer can distinguish between the egocentric and environmental orientation of the same object.

Therefore, in addition to perceiving how a figure is oriented in the environment, we should also perceive how it is oriented with respect to ourselves. If we are tilted, the figure should be perceived as oriented differently with respect to ourselves than it is with respect to the environment. It then would seem to follow that perceived egocentric orientation also ought to lead to an assignment of directions to figures, and that this would be achieved on the basis of retinal coordinates. Does this occur, and does such an assignment of directions affect phenomenal shape? The simplest way of investigating these questions is to place the figure in a horizontal plane. When a figure lies in a horizontal plane such as the floor of a room, there is no longer any basis for assignment of direction derived from gravitational information. If, furthermore, visual reference lines are eliminated by presenting the figure in a circular opening, then that source of information is also excluded. When an observer looks downward through such an opening at a novel figure lying on the floor, he immediately perceives the region that is egocentrically uppermost as the top. In other words, egocentric directions are now assigned to the figure. Here, the assignment of egocentric directions is appropriate, for under these conditions there is no other basis for assigning direction. Conversely, assigning egocentric direction is inappropriate when a figure in a vertical plane is viewed by a tilted observer, since other information about the location of top and bottom is available.

It has been possible to demonstrate that assigning egocentric directions to a figure has the same powerful impact on its phenomenal shape as do any of the already considered sources of information about phenomenal orientation. In one experiment, observers were shown fragmented figures in a horizontal plane. Unknown to them, the figures were tilted 90° from their egocentrically upright orientation (Rock & Heimer, 1957; see also Steinfeld & Greaves, 1971; Pappalardo, 1966). The figures were identified only 15% of the time, whereas they were recognized 66% of the time when they were egocentrically upright. That this effect is not the result of the retinal disorientation per se, but rather the result of the incorrect assignment of direction based on egocentric coordinates, is indicated by the results of another experiment. Here, the observers viewed upright fragmented figures when they themselves were tilted 90° from the upright. Despite a 90° retinal disorientation, the figures were recognized 51% of the time. The reason why recognition was so good in this case was that environmental directions supersede egocentric directions as the basis for assigning direction to a figure. Therefore, while there is a 15% decrement based on

retinal disorientation per se with this material, this is much less
than the decrement of 51% obtained when figures disoriented
to the same extent retinally were viewed in a horizontal plane.
The lion's share of this decrement can be safely attributed to
the incorrect assignment of directions to the figure.

Therefore, at the very first stage of processing, it seems
reasonable to assume that a figure is already differentiated with
respect to its top, bottom, and sides merely by virtue of the
orientation of its retinal image. However, as is the case with
many other kinds of perception, additional information is taken
into account, with the result that the directions for top, bottom,
and sides are assigned to a figure. These may or may not coin-
cide with the ones given to it by the retinal coordinates. When
there is no agreement between retinal and other sources of directional information, the other sources will produce a phenomenal orientation that will usually supersede and suppress
the orientation indicated by the retinal coordinates. Often,
however, when the observer is upright, all sources of information are in agreement.

To restate the argument: When a tilted observer views a figure,
there are, potentially at least, two percepts that can result. They
are illustrated in Fig. 38. These two percepts are quite different.
The one in Fig. 38a is a symmetrical figure with a ∨ balanced
on top of a horizontal base. The one in Fig. 38b is an asymmetrical

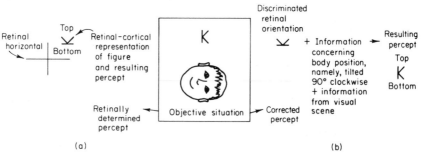

**FIG. 38**

figure with an angle touching a vertical line. However, there is good reason for believing that the retinally based percept is more or less immediately superseded by the one based on additional information about the figure's actual orientation in the environment. For us to assume that the proper orientation of objects in the world was governed by their retinal orientations would be inappropriate, inasmuch as we ourselves can change our posture. It is therefore highly adaptive to discount retinal orientation, and to decide on the basis of further information how the object is oriented in the world.

The step of shifting assigned directions from those immediately given by retinal coordinates to those based on other sources of information can be considered to be in the nature of cognitive processing. The retinally determined percept, that is, the one based on egocentric directions, may well be the primitive one—the sensory core experience—just as visual angle may be the sensory core experience in the domain of size perception. But this core percept must be set aside for one based on other information, just as is the case in size perception. The figure must be implicitly described on the basis of the shifted set of directions instead of the retinally given ones. This mental act necessitates imagining or visualizing how the figure would look were it in an upright egocentric orientation. Yet the process of reassigning directions, visualizing, and redescribing a figure (which I will refer to herein as "correction") apparently occurs successfully and almost instantaneously, to judge by the results of virtually all the experiments summarized in the previous chapters. When the observer is tilted, the figure that remains objectively upright in the test is recognized without decrement despite the altered retinal orientation. Conversely, the objectively tilted figure that preserves the retinal orientation is usually not recognized. These results establish not only that the process of correction has occurred, but also that the potential percept based on retinal orientation is superseded or suppressed.

However, it is revealing to note that a very familiar figure normally seen in one orientation, such as a single letter of the

r    ǝ    ɐ

**FIG. 39**

alphabet, does look different or odd when tilted or when the observer views it from a tilted position. When the figure is tilted, we know that it is tilted and assign directions to it accordingly. This fact is demonstrated in Fig. 39. Of course, these letters are immediately recognizable despite the tilt. This is to be expected if we assume that recognition is largely based on the corrected percept. Many of the figures used in our experiments were structurally similar to and of about the same order of complexity as the letters. There was no difficulty in recognizing them when they were retinally disoriented, that is, upright in the environment and viewed with head tilted.[2] Thus we must assume that recognition is generally governed by the corrected percept, even with letters. We did not ask our observers about such subtle aspects of their experience of the figures as "oddness," only whether they were the same figures as had been seen in the training period. The experience of "oddness" in looking at the letters in Fig. 39, however, attests to the reality of the egocentrically determined percept existing simultaneously with the corrected percept. The former is, of course, a (relatively) unfamiliar figure, whereas the latter is very familiar.

### The Conditions under Which
### a Retinal Effect Occurs

If the analysis given above is correct concerning the nature of the process that occurs when retinally disoriented figures are perceived, under what conditions should we expect difficulty in

[2]In the remainder of this chapter, unless otherwise stated, the phrase "retinally disoriented" or "retinally tilted" will mean that a figure upright in the environment is viewed by a tilted or inverted observer.

perception and recognition? We certainly should not expect that there would be any difficulty in correcting a single, relatively simple, figure. The findings reported in the previous chapters would seem to bear out this expectation.

What about complex figures? It might seem to follow that very complex figures would not be as readily recognized when retinally disoriented, because it would be more difficult to correct them. But this presupposes that every nuance and figural relation is noticed when the figure is seen in the training period. Suppose instead, given a single exposure, that only the more global characteristics of the complex figure are attended to or noted. In this event, it is plausible to think that only these features are recorded in memory.[3] Recognition in the test would then be based only on these features even when the observer remains upright, i.e., when the same retinal orientation is preserved. Therefore, perception of these same features forms the basis of recognition when the observer is tilted in the test, and since *these features* are not complex, there is no reason to predict any difference in recognition between simple and complex figures. As a matter of fact we have compared complex figures of the kind shown in Fig. 40 with the relatively simpler figures shown in Fig. 41. Although under certain conditions of training and testing—described in the Appendix (pages 144–147) —a slight retinal effect was obtained for *both* kinds of figures, there was no discernible difference in the effect obtained *between* the two kinds. Therefore, if it is the complexity of figures such as words, faces, and the like, which accounts for their being adversely affected by retinal change while most other figures are not, there must be some special sense in which they are complex that distinguishes them from material of the kind shown in Fig. 40.

One possible explanation of the adverse effect of retinal dis-

---

[3]Evidence on precisely this point has been presented by Rock, Halper, and Clayton (1972).

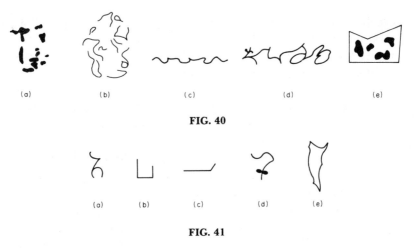

(a)            (b)            (c)            (d)            (e)

**FIG. 40**

(a)        (b)        (c)        (d)        (e)

**FIG. 41**

orientation on the recognizability of figures such as words and
faces follows from what was said above, namely, that these
figures are seen very frequently and, furthermore, that we must
learn to discriminate faces from one another and words from
one another. Therefore, we must go beyond what may have
been an initial global perception and attend to and remember
all nuances of such figures. Once that has been achieved, it becomes plausible to suppose that for such psychologically realized
complex figures, retinal disorientation would lead to real difficulty because correction must do justice to all nuances of these
figures if perceptual discrimination between similar figures is
to be maintained. We tested this deduction by comparing complex figures seen once with those seen repeatedly in training
when tested retinally upright and retinally tilted 90 or 180°.[4] In
some cases, the repeatedly seen complex figure did show a significant drop in recognition when retinally tilted, whereas those

[4]I would like to acknowledge the help of Robert Turer, Laura Vonèche, and
Charles Bebber in performing these experiments. Mr. Turer also prepared
many of the drawings of figures used in this and other experiments described
here.

seen only once did not. However, we did not always obtain this result.[5]

Some of the complex figures used in these experiments were deliberately constructed to simulate structurally printed or written words (see Fig. 40c and d). If word figures are so difficult to decode when retinally inverted, why is it that figures structurally like word figures are not reliably more difficult to recognize when retinally inverted than when retinally upright, particularly when a good deal of experience with such figures is first provided? The answer that suggested itself was that in our experiments it was possible for the observer to recognize a figure on the basis of a detail. In that event, retinal change would not produce any decrement in recognition, because correction of that detail can occur easily. With actual word figures, however, each letter must be identified and its relative position in the word must be apprehended before the word as a whole can be identified. Hence, correct recognition cannot be based merely on recognition of a part of the whole.

## AN EXPERIMENT WITH QUADRILATERAL FIGURES

Based on this analysis, we designed an experiment that would require perception of several figures at once in the test. The basic plan was as follows. The observer first saw a quadrilateral figure of the kind shown in Fig. 42. The figure was presented twice, briefly. Following the second training exposure, several test cards were shown. Each test card contained four quadrilateral figures and was exposed for 1 sec. On some of the test cards, the training figure was present (the positive cards), and

---

[5]One reason we did not may be that the repeated exposure did not lead to adequate perceptual "learning," although it did generally lead to higher recognition scores. In most of these experiments, the figures to be learned were not similar to one another, so that discrimination training was not necessary.

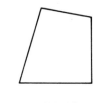

**FIG. 42**

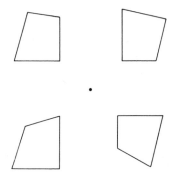

**FIG. 43**

on some it was not (the negative cards). On both types of cards the incorrect figures were similar to the training figure. The observer was required to say either "no," meaning that the training figure was not present, or he was required to indicate which figure on the card was the training figure. Figure 43 illustrates one of the positive test cards for the training figure shown in Fig. 42.

The test figures differ from one another on the basis of features that bear on direction (something that is true for many letters of the alphabet). If the observer does not adequately take into account the altered retinal orientation when he is inverted, then he could easily mistake one of them for the training figure. The observer understood that for a test figure to be correct, it had to be identical with the training figure and in the same objective orientation.

Half of the positive and half of the negative test cards were viewed with head upright, and the other half with head upside down. An observer's score was the number of test cards on which he was correct (meaning he said "no" on negative cards and selected the correct figure on the positive cards). The maximum score was 8 for the upright position and 8 for the inverted position.[6]

The mean score was 4.5 for the upright test position and 2.25 for the inverted position. The difference is substantial and significant. All but a few observers did better when upright than inverted; the results for all training figures conformed to this trend. The superiority of the upright position holds for both positive and negative cards. Although the chance of guessing correctly is high in this experiment, it is obvious that performance was well above chance, at least for the upright position.

We therefore interpret this experiment as evidence of difficulty in recognition based solely on the retinal factor. It is thus a laboratory demonstration with new material that shows a disturbance resulting only from an altered orientation of the retinal image, that approximates what is known to occur for material such as word figures and faces in daily life. In this experiment, in order to be able to respond correctly, the observer must perceive the four alternatives on each card in the brief interval allowed. They are all similar to one another, so that even when the observer is upright it is not an easy task. When inverted, however, the assignment of directions based on the egocentric coordinates—which I have suggested is the first step in the chain

[6]This research was performed by Charles Bebber and Douglas Blewett. Since it has not been published, further details of the procedure and results are given in the Appendix (pages 139–142). In certain respects, it would have been preferable to reverse the procedure and have the training cards contain multiple figures that are presented so briefly that there would not be adequate time for correction of all the figures when the observer was not upright. Then recognition for each of these figures would be subsequently tested. But this procedure does not work because, following such a brief exposure, even an upright observer is unable to hold in memory an adequate representation of each of the several figures, although we tried testing recognition at intervals as brief as 1 sec after exposure to the training card.

of events—must be discounted, and instead each figure must be corrected on the basis of information concerning where its true top, bottom, and sides are located. There is not sufficient time to do this. Furthermore, the process of correction may require focal attention, so that while correction is occurring for one figure, others that have not yet been corrected or perhaps already have been corrected, may remain in or revert back to their uncorrected state. In this state, the egocentric coordinates dominate perception. The result is that the correct figure may often not be corrected, and therefore looks different from the way it did in training; conversely, incorrect figures that are not corrected may look very much like the training figure, particularly since they were designed with this consideration in mind. An analysis of the errors bears out this prediction. When the observer was inverted, many more selections were made from just those alternatives that looked like the training figure in the inverted orientation than were made when the observer was upright. For example, for the test card shown in Fig. 43, six observers incorrectly selected the lower left alternative and six the lower right when they (the observers) were inverted; only one selected the lower left and three the lower right when upright. If the reader inverts the page, he can see how these figures may have looked to our inverted observers and then compare these impressions with the way the training figure looked when *not* inverted.

A control experiment was performed in which the same training figures were seen and the same test figures were used, except that the test figures were shown one at a time rather than four to a card.[7] Except for the specific material used, this new procedure was essentially like that of many other experiments that failed to show an effect of retinal change. With only one test figure present, it should be feasible for the inverted observer to correct the egocentrically given figural directions and arrive at the percept cor-

[7] See the Appendix (page 143) for details of this experiment.

responding to the training figure. This control experiment was necessary to determine whether the results of the main experiment were indeed based on the difficulty of correcting many figures in a limited time, as we believed, or perhaps were simply based on the nature of the material used. The mean number correct in the upright condition was 5.8; in the inverted condition it was 5.6, with the maximum score 8 in each case. Thus, there was no longer a deficit for the inverted condition, indicating that the method of testing in the main experiment entailing the exposure of several figures at once was a crucial factor.

WORD FIGURES

This experiment, which we will henceforth refer to as the quadrilateral-figure experiment, can be considered analogous to what happens when viewing inverted words of text in one important respect, namely, that here too the correction of several figures at once is required for recognition. In another respect, however, more is involved in word recognition because, in addition to letter identification, letter *order* must be taken into account. The same letters arranged differently constitute different words, so the spatial position of letters must also be a crucial part of the overall word percept. It is obvious that, viewed from an inverted position, there would be a further difficulty in correcting for letter order since the beginning letters of the word are now on the observer's right and the end letters on his left. Probably the necessity for letter correction and that of letter-order correction together account for the great difficulty of reading words of text when inverted.

Thus, our experiment pertains only to that aspect of inverted-word recognition that entails the correction of letters. It has already been noted that even a single letter, although recognizable, looks strange when disoriented. When an entire word is viewed, however, the uncorrected, egocentrically determined directions of the letters leads to nonrecognition of some and misperception of those that resemble other letters in inverted positions (*b* and *q*; *d* and *p*; *n* and *u*).[8]

Does our analysis shed any light on the even greater difficulty of deciphering inverted words cursively written? This is undoubtedly the best example of a disturbance based on disorientation of the retinal image, since inverted script is essentially not recognizable at all. There is considerable difficulty in making it out even at tilts of 90°. I believe the problem here is that, precisely because the letters are linked with one another, it is no longer clear where each letter begins and ends when the word is viewed from an inverted position. But knowing this is an essential first step in correcting each letter. Related to this is the fact that many segments in an inverted word look exactly like certain upright letters and letter combinations if they remain uncorrected, that is, are perceived on the basis of egocentric coordinates of direction. For example, in Fig. 44, which is the written word "cursive" upside down, arrows 1 and 4 point to what could be taken to be the letter *s* although arrow 1 points to the letter *i* and part of a connecting line and arrow 4 points to the letter *c*. Arrow 2 points to what looks like a *c* but is in fact an *s*, and arrow 3 points to an apparent *m* or *n* but is in fact a *u* and part of a connecting line. That misperceiving where letters begin and end is an important factor is illustrated by rewriting the word with gaps between letters or with markers between them (Fig. 45). Word identification is still difficult but, I believe, less so. In addition, many more cursively written letters resemble other letters inverted than is the case for printed letters. Finally, there is the problem of letter order. Undoubtedly all these factors interact to produce the overall difficulty.[9]

[8]The reader is referred to the Appendix (pages 150–154) for a discussion of experiments by Paul Kolers and David Perkins on speed of reading and letter naming under various kinds of orientational transformation (see also Steinfeld & Greaves, 1971).

[9]Contrast the difficulty of recognizing retinally disoriented, cursively written words with the apparent lack of difficulty in recognizing retinally disoriented script-like figures such as Fig. 40c and d (page 52). Clearly the difference, in the case of words, is the necessity of identifying all the components and their order.

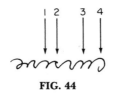

**FIG. 44**

**FIG. 45**

RECOGNITION OF FACES

Does the analysis offered here shed any light on why human faces are hard to recognize when retinally disoriented? Along with printed and written words, faces represent one of the few types of material that do look different enough to impede recognition when retinally tilted by 90° or more.

Unfortunately, we still know rather little about the perception of such a complex figure as a human face even when the face is upright. Not only do we discriminate faces from other figures, but we discriminate one face from another and one facial expression from another. There is reason for believing that these last two kinds of discrimination are the result of a good deal of prior experience. The infant at first seems to confuse one face with another, and the adult has difficulty discriminating faces among members of other races with whom he has had little contact and among members of various animal species. Given sufficient exposure to these races or species, however, discriminations can be made readily.

What is taking place during this exposure to make such discrimination possible? In studies directed at this problem, the Gibsons have concluded that the observer must learn to attend to certain features of the stimulus that, at the outset, were not noticed (Gibson & Gibson, 1955). In research conducted in our laboratory, it was shown that if a figure is complex, consisting not only of an outer contour but of internal features as well, the observer does not seem to note the internal features given only one exposure with no special instruction (Rock, Halper, & Clayton, 1972). Presumably then, although these stimulus components are registered, they do not lead to the cognitive "description" that is necessary for trace formation. These features are not adequately perceived and therefore do not leave behind adequate trace representation. However, following repeated exposure of such complex material, particularly under circumstances where attention to various features is necessary if discrimination among similar figures is to become possible, it is plausible to think that these features will be perceived and will therefore leave memory traces. A more highly articulated memory trace is thus established.

Presumably something of this sort is going on in the case of perception of faces. There are a great number of internal features and relationships among features to note: size and shape of nose; size and shape of mouth; distance between mouth and nose; distance between nose and eyes; distance between eyes; etc. Since the face is a three-dimensional object, many of these features and relationships include sizes, shapes, and distances in depth, and entail the qualities of fullness or angularity of such features. What makes a face or facial expression distinctive is its unique set of features and feature relationships.

The phenomenal appearance of each of these features and feature relationships is a function of orientation, since the phenomenal shape of all figures takes orientation into account. If any one feature, for example the nose, were seen upside down under conditions where it was not known what was being presented, it undoubtedly would look so different that it would not be recognized (see Fig. 46). If, however, the observer knew what he was looking at when he viewed the upright figure from an inverted position, then the process of correction would certainly lead to its correct perception and recognition. However, when an entire face is seen under the same conditions, the observer is confronted with a situation not unlike that of viewing a retinally inverted word. In this situation, there is a whole set of component figures and figural relationships to be corrected, and it is not possible to succeed in visualizing

**FIG. 46**

simultaneously how each of these would look were it to be egocentrically upright.

The process of correction is successful insofar as it leads to identifying the face as a face. The difficulty lies with the inability to
discriminate one face or facial expression from another, and this, I
have argued, is the end result of much prior experience. If noting
the shape of a facial feature or the precise nature of a relationship
between facial features is crucial for such discrimination, then it is
not surprising that changing the orientation of the retinal image
would lead to difficulty in distinguishing these features. As in the
case of perception of words, any component that is not undergoing
correction at a given moment will necessarily be perceived on the
basis of egocentric directions given directly by orientation of the
retinal image. For example, if the observer is concentrating on
visualizing how the mouth would look if it were to be reinverted
(Fig. 47), he may succeed in correcting it and recognizing that it has
a "smiling" configuration. Then, simultaneously with this, however, he may perceive the eye configuration shown in Fig. 48. That
is, if this part of the face were not successfully corrected at a given

FIG. 47                                             FIG. 48

moment, then it would look like a pair of strangely shaped eyes gazing upward and rightward (rather than downward and leftward, as they are). The eyes appear strangely shaped because their flatter part is on the top rather than the bottom, and they have dark markings (the eyebrows) underneath. Or conversely, if this part of the face were successfully corrected, then perhaps the mouth shown in Fig. 47 might not be. In that case, it might incorrectly appear to express sorrow rather than pleasure.

There may also be changes in three-dimensionality that are a function of the location of attached shadows. It is a fact that we interpret depth relationships revealed by shadow location on the basis of an implicit assumption that light comes from above. Thus, normally, shadow underneath a given region signifies that the region protrudes, and shadow at the top signifies that the region is indented. Under conditions of inversion, therefore, there could well be reversals of depth if shadow were the only indicator of depth. Since, however, we are dealing only with retinal inversion here, where information is available concerning the true top and bottom, and since familiarity with a face is also a source of information, complete reversals are unlikely to occur. Nevertheless, there certainly is some disturbance in the correct three-dimensional perception of the face based on the altered location of its shadows. This has a further ramification, namely, that it leads to a misperception of neutral color. A shadowed region that, upright, signifies a recession into the third dimension will retain its constancy of color to a considerable extent. But that region, seen incorrectly as in the same plane as the surrounding region, will appear darker in color (Beck, 1969).

## Is the Retinal Factor Based on
## Change of Retinal Orientation?

If impairment of recognition with retinal disorientation is a function of difficulty of correction under certain circumstances, then an effect should show up even when the observer is in the *same* orientation in the training and test periods, provided he is tilted and the figure is upright in the environment. To give an example, if one views an unfamiliar upright face from a tilted position, it will be difficult to recognize the expression and to perceive other subtle nuances which differentiate this face from others. If now that same upright face is again viewed from the same tilted position, for the same reason, the same difficulties will be encountered. Therefore, it ought to be difficult to recognize that this is the same face seen in the first exposure.

If this reasoning is correct, it means that in the experiments described in this chapter aimed at isolating the retinal factor, there are two possible bases for the decline in recognition. Typically, the procedure in these experiments consists in presenting a figure to the observer when he is in one orientation in training and in a different orientation in the test. Either the observer is upright in training and tilted in the test, or vice versa. Therefore, it has been assumed that the crucial factor here is the *change* in orientation of the retinal image of the figure. But that may or may not be what is important. When the observer is tilted and the figure is not, as is the case when the retinal factor is under study, then for the reasons already discussed, correction is necessary. Hence what may be the important factor is not so much the retinal change from training to test, but the necessity of correction in *either* training or test.

It is possible to eliminate retinal change by requiring the observer to remain tilted in the same position in both training and test. With the figure upright in the environment, correction is then necessary in both training and test, but there is no change in the orientation of the retinal image. Originally our reason for doing this kind of experiment was to control for a possible negative effect caused by the discomfort of holding the head in an abnormal position, particularly the inverted position. With no change in the observer's orientation or in the figure's orientation from training to test, we thought the only factor that might adversely affect recognition was such possible discomfort. On the whole, however, there was no adverse effect from these abnormal postures when the material tested was not of the kind that yielded a retinal effect. Only later did we realize that with material that does yield a retinal effect, this experimental procedure isolates an entirely different factor, which I call *correction*.

We have investigated this question following the general method of the quadrilateral-figure experiment. In the experiment where the observer is upright in training but rotated in the test, the assumption is that if correction fails in the test, what is perceived is not similar to what was perceived in training when correction was not necessary. If it is not similar, recognition will not occur. Suppose now that the observer is rotated in training as well. Since ample time is allowed for inspection of the figure and since only one figure at a time is shown, it may be presumed that correction occurs successfully. Nevertheless, if in the test the observer remains rotated and is given four figures at once in a brief exposure, correction should prove to be difficult, as in the main experiment. That being the case, recognition should be impaired in this condition compared to one in which the observer is upright at all times.

The procedure followed that of the main experiment, with the single exception that half the *training* figures were now seen with the observer in an inverted position. The test figures for these training figures were then also seen from this position. The remaining training figures with their test figures were all seen with the observer upright. Table 4 summarizes the various conditions. The average number of correct responses to retinally upright test cards was 4.9; for retinally inverted test cards it was 3.7. This difference is significant, although it falls short of the difference ob-

**TABLE 4**
DESIGN OF EXPERIMENT

| | 50% of figures | | Remaining 50% of figures | |
|---|---|---|---|---|
| | Training | Test | Training | Test |
| Figure | upright | upright | upright | upright |
| Observer | inverted | inverted | upright | upright |

tained in the main experiment (4.5 for upright cards and 2.25 for inverted cards).

Therefore, we can conclude that what we have been calling a retinal effect of orientation is not necessarily a function of a *change* in orientation of the retinal image from one time to another. Rather, at least in part, it is a function of non-alignment of the retinal–egocentric coordinates with the up–down, left–right coordinates of a figure determined by other information. In other words, when the directions assigned to a figure are not congruent with or aligned with the egocentric coordinate directions, correction is necessary and if, for any reason, it is not completely succesful, perception is in some sense impaired. When this is so, recognition is adversely affected.

But in the experiment just described where such a deficit was evidenced, it was not as great as when there was a *change* in retinal orientation from training to test (in the main experiment described on pages 53–56).[10] Why is this? The answer may lie with the nature of the memory traces we can assume are established in the training phase. Figure 49 schematically illustrates what may happen in

---

[10]The difference between the results of these two experiments is not quite significant. However, in a number of other experiments of various kinds not described in this monograph, it has been repeatedly found that while recognition does indeed decline when the observer is tilted in *both* training and test (as opposed to his remaining upright), it is nevertheless superior to when he is only tilted in training *or* test. Therefore, it can be safely assumed that there is a real advantage when the subject is in the *same* tilted position throughout. The speculations that follow attempt to explain this fact.

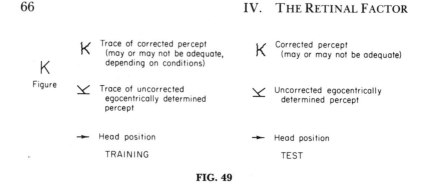

FIG. 49

training and test when the observer is in the *same* tilted position in both. Some trace is, of course, left of the percept arrived at on the basis of correction. It may or may not be an adequate trace, depending upon whether or not the correction was fully succesful. In addition, however, there may also be a trace of the egocentrically determined percept even though it is a percept that is more or less superseded.

Therefore, in the test, if we assume there are again two percepts, there are two possible bases for recognition, since each of these percepts can be said to be identical to or similar to its corresponding trace.

Figure 50 schematically illustrates what may happen when there is a change in the observer's orientation from training to test. The situation in training is identical to the case just considered and so, therefore, are the memories presumed to be established. But in the

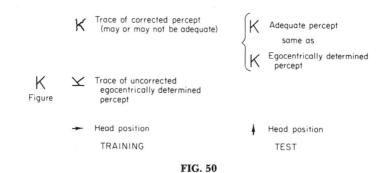

FIG. 50

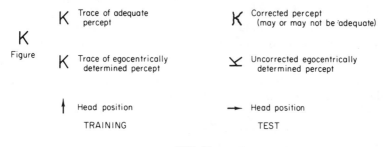

**FIG. 51**

test, there is now only one percept (since the figure perceived on the basis of assignment of directions is the same as that determined by the subject's egocentric coordinates), and that is fully adequate. There is, therefore, no possibility of recognition being aided by the second egocentrically determined trace, because that is different from the corresponding percept now generated by the test stimulus.

Figure 51 illustrates the converse situation, namely, where the observer is upright in training and tilted in the test. Here again, recognition can only occur for the corrected percept. There is no trace corresponding to the uncorrected, egocentrically determined, percept that occurs in the test.

Therefore, when there is retinal change from training to test, the observer is deprived of the possibility of recognizing on the basis of similarity between the uncorrected percept and trace. When there is no retinal change, the observer has a dual basis for recognition. The question then arises as to why recognition is not better in this situation (as outlined in Fig. 49) and, in fact, is poorer than in the situation where the observer is upright throughout, since in the latter case there is really only one percept and one trace possible? The answer surely must be that the combined effectiveness of a trace left by a percept resulting from correction and a trace left by an uncorrected, more or less superseded, egocentrically determined percept is not equal to that of a trace of a percept that does not require correction at all.

To sum up then, I have suggested the following account of the retinal factor: certain materials are difficult to perceive and recognize when the orientation of the retinal image is not egocentrically upright, that is, when the directions assigned to the figure are not congruent with the egocentric directions. The difficulty stems from the necessity of suppressing the percept based on egocentric directions, and imagining how the figure would look on the basis of the directions assigned to it. That being the case, the essential fact is the lack of congruence between assigned and egocentric coordinate directions, and not the change in the orientation of the retinal image from one time to another if such change should occur. Therefore the essential meaning of the term "retinal disorientation" used throughout this chapter is not change of retinal orientation from one occasion to another, but the departure from egocentric uprightness. Recognition is somewhat better in experiments where correction is necessary but where there is no change of retinal orientation from training to test, as compared to the case where there is such change. This is probably the result of the facilitating effect of a secondary percept, namely, the uncorrected egocentrically determined percept and its trace, which just happen in this special case to remain identical to one another.

## Recognition as a Function
## of Degree of Retinal Disorientation

What is the relationship between degree of retinal disorientation and recognizability for material that *does* show an effect of retinal disorientation? Earlier, this question was investigated for change of assigned directions, with retinal orientation held constant. It was found that every figure is unique in the manner in which its shape is altered by shifting its directions through varying degrees. However, shifts of 45 and 90° generally led to at least as much as and, more often than not, a greater change than shifts of 180°. Now, the facts concerning effect of degree of tilt must be established for retinal orientation per se. Follow-

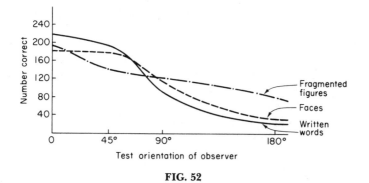

**FIG. 52**

ing that, one must consider how the theoretical analysis presented here would account for the facts.

As has already been mentioned, informal observation with material such as word figures and faces indicates increasing difficulty with increasing tilt. We confirmed this experimentally.[11] The observers were briefly shown cursively written words, faces of famous people (from which distinguishing features that were likely to permit easy recognition, such as hair in one case, were removed) and fragmented figures. Each observer saw several examples of each type of material when he was upright, when his head was tilted 45° clockwise, 90° clockwise, and inverted. The figures were always upright. The task was to identify each figure. Because familiar material was being tested, a training period was not necessary. Figure 52 plots the number of recognitions against degree of change of retinal orientation. It is perfectly clear that recognition of the material tested is a decreasing function of degree of retinal disorientation.

The question arises as to whether novel material will conform to this same trend, and the answer is theoretically quite important. To investigate this question, we repeated the quadrilateral-figure experiment with only one change. We substituted a 90° head tilt for the inverted head condition. The mean

[11]This experiment was conducted by George Steinfeld. See the Appendix (page 147) for further details. See also Steinfeld (1970) and Steinfeld and Greaves (1971).

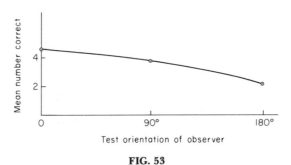

FIG. 53

score was 4.7 for the upright test condition and 3.8 for the 90°
tilted condition. Thus there is a significant drop in recognition
in the tilted condition, but the magnitude of the effect is less
than that obtained in the condition where the observers were inverted. If we plot the recognition score for the novel material
used in these two experiments for the three retinal orientations
tested, we obtain the same decreasing function as we had for
familiar material (Fig. 53). This finding would seem to support
the belief that the quadrilateral-figure experiment does succeed
in simulating the conditions that give rise to difficulty in recognition with familiar material as a result of retinal disorientation.

How can we interpret the finding that the greater the degree
of retinal disorientation, the more difficult the recognition?
One obvious explanation relevant to the results with familiar
material is simply that we have had relatively little experience
with retinal inversion based on inversion of the head, somewhat
more experience with tilts of 90°, and a fair amount of experience with lesser head tilts in the neighborhood of 45°. We
often view things with slight tilts of the head, but hardly ever
with the head inverted.[12]

---

[12]This argument would not apply as clearly if we included situations where the
object is disoriented rather than ourselves, because we often do see printed
or written material or the like that is inverted with respect to ourselves, as in
seeing a book on the table. What the frequency is for varying degrees of disorientation considered in this way is not known.

The experience hypothesis, however, begs the question because the experience must result in successful recognition on each occasion before it can be credited with contributing toward subsequent recognizability. One could look at an inverted word for the longest time without this "experience" being of any value for future recognition, unless during that period it was ultimately recognized. Therefore, if the more frequent prior experience we have had with certain material when the head is only slightly tilted is the reason it is fairly easy to recognize such material now, then those prior experiences must have led to easy recognition, too. So we are back where we started from. Why is recognition easier in the first place for only slight degrees of retinal change?

Logical considerations alone, however, are rarely convincing. This is why it was of theoretical importance to determine the nature of the function for novel material. The results shown in Fig. 53 do indicate that recognition is a decreasing function of degree of retinal disorientation for novel material as well. Therefore, it is entirely probable that the same mechanism explains the function obtained for familiar material.

In terms of the theoretical analysis of the retinal factor presented earlier, the explanation would have to be sought in the difficulty of correcting a retinally disoriented figure. It would have to be argued that the process of correction becomes increasingly difficult as the degree of disorientation of the image becomes greater. Why should this be so? The fact that a rotation of 180° would be particularly troublesome seems to follow from the analysis. The region of the figure that is egocentrically the "top" must be corrected to "bottom" and vice versa; the region that is egocentrically "left" must be corrected to "right" and vice versa. In other words, the diametric opposition that arises in the case of 180° rotation between egocentrically governed directions and those assigned to a figure ought to prove difficult to deal with.

A related factor in the case of material such as words and faces is that when egocentrically *inverted,* certain features in the uncorrected egocentric orientation can plausibly represent features of the object in question. As a result, the egocentrically determined percept may tend to endure and not be as readily suppressed. For example, eyes are still "eyes" upside down because they remain side by side; a mouth is still a "mouth" because its long axis is still horizontal; the letters in a word can become other letters, and the array of letters still has a side-by-side arrangement. This is not true at other tilts, such as 90°.

Granted then that these considerations in part account for the great difficulty with rotations of 180° or inversions, what more general explanation can be offered for the increasing difficulty of recognition as a function of degree of retinal disorientation? In order to describe the figure on the basis of its true top, bottom, and sides, the observer must do the following:

1. Ignore the description that stems from the directions given by the egocentric coordinates.
2. Visualize how the figure would look if it were egocentrically upright, that is, if the region that is tagged "top" by gravitational and other information were egocentrically uppermost, rather than "left" or "right" or "lowermost" as it now is.

To visualize it egocentrically upright necessitates turning it around mentally. We know nothing about such mental processes, but as a hypothesis, I would suggest that visualizing a figure in a different orientation from the one it is in occurs literally by rotating the figure in one's imagination by degrees until it has arrived at the desired orientation, or by visualizing the transformations the figure would undergo in its egocentric appearance as one turns by degrees until one arrives at the desired orientation. (Of the two, visualizing the self turning seems easier and more natural to me.) In other words, I am suggesting that we can arrive at the desired correction only by visualizing the transition to it. The greater the degree of angular change involved, the more taxing it is on the imagination, because the figure must be visualized as it undergoes a longer sequence of transformations.

**FIG. 54**                                    **FIG. 55**

An example may help give the reader an intuitive understanding of the matter. Suppose the observer views Fig. 54 (one of the training figures used in the quadrilateral-figure experiment). The reader may find it helpful to place this page in an upright position and view it first with head tilted 90° counterclockwise. In that position the retinal image falls in such an orientation as to lead to the percept shown in Fig. 55, if egocentric orientation based on retinal coordinates alone governs the outcome. The observer must ignore this percept, however, and go on to describe the figure on the basis of where he knows its top, bottom, and sides to be. Thus, the description would have to include the fact that the figure rests on a point at the bottom left, that its left side slopes inward as it ascends, and that its top is almost horizontal. This description adds up to a very different figure from the percept evoked on the basis of the egocentric coordinates. For this reason, some difficulty is involved in ignoring or suppressing the latter and substituting the former. However, it is not too difficult to arrive at the new description. In visualizing how the figure would look if the head were to be tilted back to the upright, it is apparent that the bottom is a long line sloping up toward the right, and so forth.

Next consider the case where the observer's head is upside down, and he is viewing Fig. 54. (The reader is invited to try this out.) Egocentric coordinates lead to the percept shown in Fig. 56. Again, the observer must ignore this percept, and go on to describe the figure in terms appropriate to its true top and bottom, left and right sides. As the reader-observer will appreciate, it is more difficult to visualize how the figure would look and therefore more difficult to arrive at the correct description. Left–right reversals are

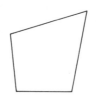

**FIG. 56**

particularly troublesome. Not only will the egocentric left side become the right side of the corrected percept and vice versa, but the slope of these sides will change as well. The left side in the egocentric percept (Fig. 56) slopes upward and to the left, whereas the left side in the corrected percept slopes upward and to the right (Fig. 54), and so forth.

The hypothesis suggested above—that the correction process for retinally disoriented figures is more difficult for greater degrees of retinal disorientation because the observer must mentally rotate the perceived figure from its egocentrically given orientation to the desired orientation—has two implications. One is that the greater the magnitude of rotation required, the longer it should take to achieve mental rotation. The other is that a similar function should be obtained for mental rotation of figures of all kinds, for example, rotation of three-dimensional figures about a vertical axis.

Both implications have been shown to be correct in an experiment published after the first draft of this manuscript was completed (Shepard & Metzler, 1971). The investigators required their subjects to judge whether the members of a pair of perspective line drawings, such as those shown in Fig. 57, were the same as one another though differently oriented, or different from one another. For half of the "same" pairs, the two drawings differed from one another by a rotation in the picture plane; for the other half, they differed by a rotation in depth. Varying degrees of difference in orientation were tested, from 0 to 180°, in 20° steps. The results, plotting mean reaction time for the "same" pairs against the angle of rotation, are shown in Fig. 58.

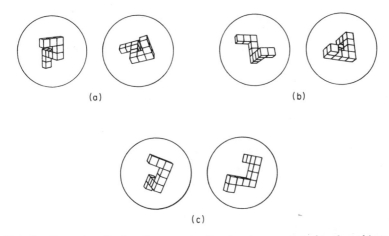

(a)    (b)

(c)

**FIG. 57** Examples of pairs of perspective line drawings presented to the subjects: (a) a "same" pair, which differs by an 80° rotation in the picture plane; (b) a "same" pair, which differs by an 80° rotation in depth; (c) a "different" pair, which cannot be brought into congruence by *any* rotation. (Reproduced from R. N. Shepard and J. Metzler, Mental rotation of three-dimensional objects, *Science*, 1971, **170** (No. 3972), 702, Fig. 1.)

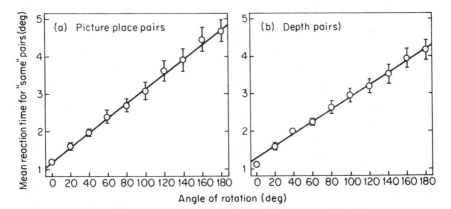

**FIG. 58** Mean reaction times to two perspective line drawings portraying objects of the same three-dimensional shape. Times are plotted as a function of angular difference in portrayed orientation: (a) for pairs differing by a rotation in the picture plane only; (b) for pairs differing by a rotation in depth. (The centers of the circles indicate the means and, when they extend far enough to show outside these circles, the vertical bars around each circle indicate a conservative estimate of the standard error of that mean based on the distribution of the eight component means contributed by the individual subjects.) (Reproduced from R. N. Shepard and J. Metzler, Mental rotation of three-dimensional objects, *Science*, 1971, **170** (No. 3972), 702, Fig. 2.)

It can be seen that reaction time is a linear function of the angular difference between the two figures, and this is true for rotations in the plane and for rotations in depth. It requires only about 1 sec to judge that two such figures are the same when they are in the same orientation, but it takes more than 4 sec to do so when they differ from one another by 180°. Since the difficulty of visualizing a figure in an orientation different from the one it is in is thus seen to be a function of the angular difference between the two, it seems very plausible to conclude that precisely this kind of mental process is involved in the perception of retinally disoriented figures. The investigators were not concerned with this particular phenomenon, nor do they even refer to it, but their findings make it possible to view it as a manifestation of a broader principle of mental functioning.

The greater difficulty in correcting figures that are rotated 180° may explain a finding mentioned in an earlier chapter. When an inverted observer views drawings such as those in Fig. 10 (Chapter II, page 13) they almost always recognize the face that is retinally upright rather than the face that is environmentally upright. Presumably, in such figures, the first thing to happen is that recognition of the inverted face occurs on the basis of the egocentrically determined up–down direction. Once that occurs, it is plausible to think that recognition of the other, environmentally upright, face is blocked. Recognition of one alternative stabilizes that alternative at the expense of the other. Thus the victor in this contest is the percept that is linked to the egocentrically determined set of directions rather than the percept that is linked to the corrected set of directions. The misperception of an upright *b* as a *q* or a *d* as a *p* when viewed from an inverted posture would seem to illustrate the same effect.

The question then arises as to why the retinally upright figure was not favored in the experiment described earlier and illustrated in Fig. 11 (page 13), since this experiment also makes use of ambiguous figures. There, it was the environmentally upright alternative that was recognized most of the time. The essential difference between that experiment and those using faces is the magnitude of separation between the "tops" of the two alternatives, namely, 90° versus 180°. This suggests that where correction is very difficult, the retinally determined percept tends to endure to a greater extent than when correction is not too difficult. Consequently, the retinally determined percept is not suppressed, or not immediately suppressed, with the result that it becomes the organization which is selected in an ambiguous figure.

Another finding fits this interpretation. An experiment was performed in which the upright observer first saw in training, figures such as the one shown in Fig. 12 (page 15). In a recognition test, he was briefly shown an array of figures such as that illustrated in Fig. 59 and had to indicate which of these was familiar. The observer himself is tilted in the test and in the particular variation now being described, his head was, in fact, upside down. Note that the critical figure seen in training appears twice on the card (although the observer does not know this), once upright and once rotated 180°. The result was that observers chose each of these critical figures about equally often. Yet in an experiment identical to this one but with only a 90° tilt of the observer's head in the test and a corresponding 90° tilt of one of the two critical figures (the other remaining upright), there was a very significant favoring of the upright critical figure.

There is reason for thinking that this particular method of testing is a factor in the outcome. If instead of testing in the manner

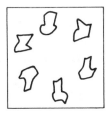

**FIG. 59**

described, the test figures are briefly shown one at a time, with the task of the observer to indicate which are familiar and which are not, then, by and large, there is no significant drop in recognition of figures of this kind which remain upright when viewed from an inverted position of the head. When only the upright test figure is seen by the inverted observer, he carries out the correction despite the difficulty and ignores the *unfamiliar* retinally determined percept. But when he has a choice and when one of the alternatives is a retinally upright version of the figure seen in training, which perhaps an observer happens to notice first, recognition occurs and that figure is selected.

There is one further point to be made about the finding of increasing difficulty of recognition with increasing degree of retinal disorientation. If the analysis made in a previous section (pages 63–68) is correct, the essential factor is the increasing disparity between assigned and egocentrically determined directions, and not the increasing disparity between previous and present retinal orientations. In other words, if the former factor is isolated, so that there is no change in retinal orientation between a training and test exposure, then we may predict that the same relationship between degree of retinal disorientation and recognition will be obtained. This prediction is confirmed by some results of an experiment not yet mentioned. In the experiment (described in detail in the Appendix, pages 144–147) many figures were shown in training, and each later had to be selected from among several similar alternatives. All combinations of the following training and test orientations of the subject were employed: 0, 45, 90, and 180°. Thus, among all these combinations, there were four conditions where the subject was in the *same* orientation in training and test: 0–0°; 45–45°; 90–90°; and 180–180°. The results for these conditions, expressed in terms of percentage of correct recognitions, and taking recognition in the 0–0° as a base line, were respectively

100, 91, 86, and 65%. Thus, the progressive decrease in recognition with increasing retinal disorientation is obtained under these conditions, entailing *no* retinal *change* at all.[13]

[13]What contribution, if any, might we expect *change* of retinal orientation alone to make from training to rest in the obtained relationship between degree of disorientation and recognition? It is not possible to isolate change of retinal orientation per se from the factor of congruency of egocentrically determined and assigned directions, because whenever retinal orientation is changed, it changes *ipso facto* the orientation of the image with respect to the egocentric coordinates. But from the standpoint of logical analysis, one can argue that greater degrees of retinal change per se would not lead to greater difficulty in recognition. The reader may recall that the superior recognition obtained in experiments in which the subject's orientation does not change from training to test (but where he is disoriented in both) in comparison to those where it does change (pages 63–68) was attributed to the facilitating effect of identity between a secondary, uncorrected percept and trace based on this uncorrected percept. If true, then to put the matter the other way around, the poorer performance where retinal change does occur is the result of the difference between the two uncorrected, egocentrically determined percepts, of which one takes place during training and the other during the test. When a difference exists between the two percepts, recognition cannot be facilitated by any communication between the uncorrected trace from the training period and the uncorrected percept at the time of the test. The point I now wish to add is that there is no reason to believe that the degree of such difference is a function of the degree of retinal change from training to test. In fact, to the contrary, we know from the analysis of the assignment of direction factor that a shift of 45° in assigned directions is as likely to produce a marked phenomenal change in a figure's appearance, if not more so, as a shift of 180°.

CHAPTER V

# Discussion

## Theories about Orientation of Form

There have been surprisingly few theoretical attempts to explain the facts about orientation in form perception, and few existing principles seem applicable to this topic. In what follows, I will consider the attempts at theorizing that have been made under these headings: elementaristic theories, the Gestalt theory, feature analysis theories, empiristic theories, and direction-of-scanning theories.

### ELEMENTARISTIC THEORIES

Ernst Mach (1914) implied that a form reduces to the component sensations of line-direction of which it is constituted. Therefore, if its orientation is changed, it looks quite different, but if its orientation is unchanged and it is transposed in size, it will look quite similar. Rotating a figure by 180° would have less effect on its appearance than would some lesser degree of rotation, because each line would then return to its initial orientation. Presumably, then, a tilt of 90° would introduce the maximum change, although Mach did not himself explicitly draw this conclusion. However, for Mach, sensations of space were closely connected with motor processes, particularly of the eye muscles. Since the motor apparatus of the eyes is symmetrical with respect to the median plane of the head, this results in great similarity between visual sensations that are symmetrical with respect to a vertical axis. Because of the absence of any corresponding up–down symmetry in the motor apparatus of the eyes and the reaction to gravity of the motor apparatus of the rest of the body, visual sensations that are symmetrical about a horizontal axis are experienced as different, not similar. These considerations lead to the following additional conclusions: Figures that are mirror images (left–right reversals) of one another will look alike and will be easily confused with one another; figures that are turned upside down (rotated 180°) will look different because of the up–down change, but, as already noted, they will look similar because the orientation of each component line sensation is not changed.

Whereas some of our findings substantiate Mach's theory, others do not. Inversions, in contrast to 180° rotations, do introduce large shifts in the orientation of many component lines of a figure, but have phenomenal effects very similar to 180° rotations. Also, we have seen that the effect of altered orientation is a function of the unique characteristics of the specific figure. As far as Mach's theory of sensation is concerned, presumably the sensation of a line in a given orientation is a function of the orientation of its retinal image. Yet, we now know that, given correction, the orientation of the image of most figures can be changed with little if any effect on the appearance of the figure. Conversely, with no change in the orientation of the image, a figure will look very different if the assignment of directions to it is altered—an effect demonstrated even with Mach's own example of the square–diamond figure (pages 15–16). Whereas Mach was right about the great similarity of left–right reversed figures to their originals, this similarity is not based on the symmetry of the retinal images about the sagittal plane of the head (which Mach thought derived from symmetry of the motor apparatus of the eyes), but on perceived symmetry about a phenomenally vertical axis. A left–right reversal of a figure will continue to look strikingly similar to the original, even if it is viewed with head tilted 90°.

Mach did not seem to realize that such an atomistic theory of form as the sum of all the component line sensations cannot do justice to the facts. For example, according to Mach, a figure rotated by 180° should look *unchanged*—not merely similar—for the reason stated earlier, namely, that the orientation of each line remains unchanged. To speak of gravity-determined up–down asymmetry as an explanation of the profound change in appearance of such rotated figures is to fail to see that it is only in the directional *relationship* of one part of a figure to others that rotation can be said to introduce change. That is, although every line component of a figure rotates back to its original orientation when it is upside down, the directional "sense" of that line is inverted. In other words, the upper or leftmost part of that line becomes the lower or rightmost part of it when it is upside down. This "sense" is given by the phenomenal orientation of the figure as a whole.

A modern variant of Mach's theory derives from the work of Hubel and Wiesel, in which cortical cells have been discovered which respond only when the retina is stimulated by contours in specific orientations (Hubel & Wiesel, 1962). One might think that the perception of a figure could be reduced to the firing of those cells that "detect" the orientation of each of its line components. Changing the figure's orientation results in the stimulation of a whole new set of such cells, and hence in an entirely different percept.

The criticism made of Mach's theory applies here as well. These detector mechanisms certainly cannot be thought of as determining the phenomenal orientations of lines in the environment, since constancy (or correction) is achieved when the head is tilted.

Of course it could be argued that these cells detect the perceived egocentric orientation of lines, and that changing the retinal orientation by tilting one's head does result in a changed percept *prior to correction*. While there may be some merit in this formulation, it has little bearing on the facts about orientation in form perception.[1] We have seen that the most general principle about changes in perceived form is that a figure will look different if there is a change in the location of the directions top, bottom, and sides assigned to it. Thus extreme change can occur even where there is no change in retinal orientation, and typically, no change will occur even with great change in retinal orientation. In the few cases where change of retinal orientation per se does lead to altered perception (words, faces, and the like) we have seen that the effect is related to the presence of multiple subsidiary figures or figure relationships. Each of the component letters of a word can easily be corrected.

## GESTALT THEORY

By and large Gestalt theory was designed to do justice to all those facts which indicate that perception corresponds to the relationship among parts of the retinal image rather than to absolute properties of the image. For example, a figure can be transposed in size without changing its phenomenal shape. From this point of view, a change in orientation should not affect shape either, because there is no change in the relationship among parts of a figure with respect to one another. However, the relationship

[1] If the firing of these cells explained perceived egocentric orientation, one would expect a degree of precision that in fact does not exist. A line oriented anywhere between 5° clockwise and 5° counterclockwise from the sagittal axis of the head may appear parallel to the long axis of the head (see Rock, 1954). Furthermore, prism adaptation to altered egocentric orientation is possible (see Mack & Rock, 1968) so that, following adaptation, only a line whose image is *tilted* from the retinal vertical axis will appear egocentrically "vertical." Therefore, the only defensible conclusion about these cells would seem to be that they provide a basis for discriminating one orientation from another, rather than that they are directly the correlate of any kind of phenomenal orientation.

between figure and background changes when its orientation is altered.

There are some indications that Gestaltists thought along these lines. For example, Kopfermann (1930) demonstrated that whether a square-shaped figure looks like a square or a diamond is not so much a function of the absolute orientation of its retinal image as it is a function of the orientation of its image relative to its background frame of reference. If the frame of reference and inner figure are both tilted as in Fig. 60a and c, then the inner figure looks much the way it does when it is not tilted, namely, in Fig. 60a it appears similar to 60b, and in Fig. 60c it resembles 60d. Koffka (1935) explicitly stated that "orientation, as a factor which determines the shape of . . . figure, is, then, not an absolute matter, but relative with regard to the frame [p. 185]."

The most penetrating analysis of the problem of orientation to date was made by Erich Goldmeier (1937), a student of Wertheimer, as part of a study of the nature of similarity in form perception. Goldmeier demonstrated that the orientation of figures with respect to the vertical and horizontal axes of space was crucial: that the parts of a figure take on significance in relation to these axes. For example, whether a line of a figure is seen as a "base" depends on its alignment with the horizontal of space. He further observed that although the vertical axis separates equal "halves" of space, left and right, the horizontal axis separates unequal halves, top

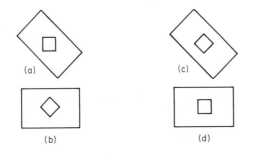

**FIG. 60**

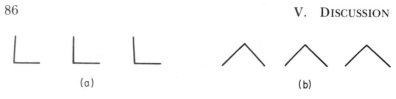

(a)                                  (b)

**FIG. 61**

and bottom. It is for this reason that symmetry about a vertical axis is phenomenally "realized," whereas symmetry about an axis in any other direction may not be. He demonstrated this fact experimentally.

Another manifestation noted by Goldmeier of the *prägnanz* or singularity of the horizontal and vertical axes is the fact that right angles can easily be discriminated from angles slightly smaller or larger *only* if the sides are horizontal and vertical, as shown in Fig. 61. In Fig. 61a one quickly sees that the right angle is in the middle, in Fig. 61b one is not sure which it is.

These ideas are, therefore, highly compatible with the general Gestalt theory of perception. However, Köhler (1940) came to the conclusion (based on the experiment described in Chapter II) that it was not relative orientation but absolute retinal orientation that mattered as far as difficulty in the recognition of disoriented figures was concerned. Thus, he felt compelled to offer an explanation that would deal with such facts without at the same time overthrowing the relational approach to most other facts of perception. He suggested that a directional gradient exists in the tissue of the visual cortex. If in Fig. 62 this gradient is represented by the plus–minus polarity, then it is clear that, while the internal relationships among the parts of the letter A are invariant for all orientations, the external relationships of the figure to the gradient vary. On the left, the apex of the A points in the minus direction of the gradient, and on the right, it points in the plus direction.

The explanations of the effect of changes in orientation presented

$$- \qquad\qquad\qquad -$$

A                     ∀

$$+ \qquad\qquad\qquad +$$

**FIG. 62**

here are quite compatible with the basic ideas of Gestalt psychology. Given the emphasis in Gestalt thinking on *relationships*, it would be strange if the phenomenal shape of a figure was not affected by its orientation in relation to the background. Thus it might be taken to be implicit in Gestalt theory that what matters is perceived orientation rather than the orientation of the retinal image. Kopfermann's demonstration (Fig. 60) points in this direction. But except for Köhler's work, there was no direct test of this question.

We now know that Köhler was not correct in believing that it was exclusively change of retinal orientation per se that led to change in phenomenal shape. Thus all the data presented in this monograph on change that is based on incorrect assignment of directions do not in any way require a theory such as the one Köhler thought was necessary. Only in special cases where change of retinal orientation per se does affect recognition could it even be applicable. However, if a simple figure such as a square continues to look like a square even when viewed with head tilted—so that its image is now a diamond—then apparently it cannot be the case that the altered orientation of the cortical representation of the retinal image within the hypothetical gradient is the basis for the change of appearance from square to diamond. If a gradient existed, it would affect simple figures as well as complex ones.

To the extent that correction is successful with retinal change only, there is transposition of orientation. In other words, orientation of the retinal image can be altered *without* altering phenomenal shape, as can size and position. Therefore, the Gestalt emphasis on the transposability of forms receives further support from our findings, rather than a challenge, as Köhler himself had thought.

FEATURE ANALYSIS THEORIES

Attempts have been made to design machines that can "recognize" patterns on the basis of features. Thus, for example, the letter A has two oblique lines and one horizontal line. Obviously then if some features are defined in terms of orientation, "recognition" must fail if a letter is disoriented.

To get around this difficulty one can try to design the machine in such a way that letters are first normalized with respect to orientation before the process of feature analysis begins. But for the machine to know how to normalize a form presupposes its prior "recognition." Another method is to eliminate orientation of features as a criterion. For example, the letter A is analyzed as containing three straight lines whereas the letter D has one straight and one curved line. There are many problems with this method but I would like to call attention to one in particular. These attempts to cope with the problem of orientation change assume that human beings *do* recognize disoriented letters. It is true that they can and often do so, but letter and word recognition is a special case because the observer is aware of the disorientation and is seeking to correct for it. The major fact about orientation change, however, is that without knowledge of the change, form orientation and recognition *are modified.* Therefore, if machines are designed to allow for "recognition" of disoriented figures, they will ipso facto not do justice to the major fact of nonrecognition by human beings of disoriented figures. The converse is obviously also true.

One theory which did address the problem of the effect of orientation on form perception was advanced by Sutherland (1957a, b). It was based on the experimental finding that in the octopus and goldfish (as in the young child), discrimination of oblique rectangles sloping to the left or right is extremely difficult, while discrimination of a horizontal from a vertical rectangle is relatively easy. Sutherland reasoned that the nervous system in such species analyzes for vertical and horizontal retinal extent, but not for other inclinations. The ratio of vertical to horizontal extent would be identical for oblique rectangles at 45 or 135°, and thus it would be difficult to discriminate two such rectangles from one another.[2]

---

[2]Sutherland (1963a, b) later advanced a different theory about this problem which incorporated recent physiological findings concerning the relative number of cells in the visual system of various species sensitive to contours in different retinal orientations.

This hypothesis is based on the assumption that these orientations are defined in terms of retinal coordinates. The question therefore arises as to whether an animal would still find it easier to discriminate a horizontal from a vertical rectangle than one oblique rectangle from another, differently oriented, oblique rectangle, even if the animal itself were inclined 45° with respect to gravity.[3] I am reasonably sure that this would be true for children. We now know it is true for adults (Attneave & Olson, 1967). If this proves to be generally true, a theory based on analysis of the horizontal and vertical retinal dimensions of form would not do justice to the facts.

These findings in animals and children can be understood in terms of certain psychological principles discussed previously. Oblique clockwise and counterclockwise rectangles are very similar phenomenally because they are both, cognitively speaking, "oblique rectangles at a given angle to the vertical and horizontal." Only the inclusion of left and right directions in the cognitive description would make it possible to distinguish them. In other words, the subject in a discrimination learning task must arrive at the rule "X means reward; Y does not." If X and Y are mental representatives of oblique rectangles, they are not apt to contain any reference to clockwise or counterclockwise orientation. Therefore, as mental representatives, they are essentially the same. (Of course, if both rectangles were simultaneously present, it would be immediately evident that their slants differed *from one another*.)

Other figures that are mirror images of one another (left–right reversals) are also difficult to discriminate, including figures that do not contain oblique line components. Young children cannot learn to discriminate figures such as ⊂ from ⊃. Horizontal and vertical rectangles, on the other hand, are, cognitively speaking, very different. Also "top" and "bottom" are very different; hence,

---

[3]To my knowledge, no test of the effect of retinal disorientation per se has ever been made with animals. If animals are less capable of correction and react in terms of the more primitive egocentric system of directionalization, then retinal change may lead to phenomenal change even for simple figures. If so, however, it would be quite maladaptive, since animals often change their position in space.

it is easy for children and adults to learn to discriminate figures
that are rotated 180° or inverted. The young child easily dis-
criminates ∪ from ∩.

## EMPIRISTIC THEORY

Although no theorist in recent times has suggested it, the attempt
might be made to explain the facts about orientation in terms of
specific past experience. Only those figures typically seen in one
orientation are difficult to recognize in a new orientation. Figures
that are seen in daily life in all orientations are of course equally
well recognized in all orientations. So one might say that recognition is poor for disoriented figures because they have not been
experienced in the new orientations.

However, such an explanation completely begs the question
of why a figure seen previously in only one orientation should
look different and not be recognized in a new orientation. In experiments with novel material, there is usually no practice with the
figure in training in a given orientation, only a single exposure.
The purpose of this exposure, of course, is merely to provide one
percept to compare with that of the same figure in a new orientation.
One could just as well present the same figure simultaneously in
two orientations. If the observer remains naïve, the two figures
would look different to him. Goldmeier (1937) has used this
technique. Here it seems inappropriate to speak of past experience
at all.

If perception were such that only identical stimuli falling in the
same retinal locus looked the same, then orientation change would
not be a special case requiring explanation. If it were the case
that figures whose images were changed in *any* respect were not
recognizable, then, of course, recognition would require specific
past experience with every figure in every conceivable location,
size, or distance. Since, however, this is not the case, and instead
transposability is the rule, the question legitimately arises, why does
novelty of orientation lead to altered perception? In other words,

why shouldn't a figure look much the same in all orientations, so that past experience with it in all orientations would not be necessary for recognition?

Furthermore, we now know that it is generally not true that the orientation of the *retinal image* must remain the same for recognition to occur. On the contrary, a figure will almost always be recognized regardless of the fact that the retinal image falls in a new orientation, provided that there is no change in assignment of directions.

Where retinal change alone occurs, and material such as words or faces *is* difficult to recognize, it is clear that past experience is a factor. Only by virtue of considerable experience with figures such as words and faces are we able to perceive all the parts and their relationships in a single glance. For this reason change of retinal orientation can play havoc with material of this kind. So, past experience is very relevant, but it hardly makes sense to say that it explains this effect. The past experience here has the role of enabling perceptual discriminations to be made, but that does not imply that it is the absence of such experience with such material in other retinal orientations which explains the difficulty in perceiving it in these orientations. Rather the difficulty resides in the necessity for correction.

But, one may ask, isn't it true that when we do obtain experience with material such as word figures in different retinal orientations recognition becomes quite good? It is also probable that we see such material more frequently in slightly tilted retinal orientations —for example, when our head is not perfectly upright—than in very tilted orientations. Some might think that this fact could explain the functions shown in Fig. 52 (Chapter IV, page 69) in which recognition of such material declines with increasing retinal disorientation.

However, it is worth repeating that, if experience in abnormal orientations is to permit correct perception at a later time, it must result in successful recognition during these encounters. In fact, perhaps no amount of experience with inverted words or faces will ever lead to the kind of perception that takes place when these figures are retinally upright. If the figure is such that the correction process cannot cope with it, then all that may happen with repeated exposure to it is that *this* percept (in its uncorrected form) may become very familiar, and an association between this percept and the object it is known to represent will develop. Naturally, then, experience with printed words, pictures of faces, and the like in various orientations under conditions where we can check what the figures actually are will enable us to recognize them more easily in such orientations. This may explain the finding that 180° rotation leads to better recognition performance than, say, inversion, since the former is occasionally experienced whereas the latter almost never (Kolers, 1968; Kolers & Perkins, 1969a, b). In this sense, past experience may affect recognition of retinally disoriented figures.[4] In any case, an alternative explanation of the function shown in Fig. 52 has been suggested, namely, that the task of visualizing a figure in a different egocentric orientation is more difficult for greater degrees of tilt. The fact that a similar function was obtained for new material (Fig. 53) supports this second explanation. Also, a similar function was obtained when there was *no change* of retinal orientation from training to test (pages 78–79).

So much for the notion that the lack of specific experience with particular forms in every orientation can explain failure to recognize them in novel orientations. It is possible that past experience plays a more general role, such as giving rise to the very tendency to assign directions to figures or improving our ability to correct disoriented figures. But there is as yet no evidence on these questions. The possible role of past experience in the origin of the egocentric coordinates is discussed in a following section: "the issue of adaptation to a disoriented retinal image" (pages 102–105).

In the case of objects seen in daily life in all orientations, one might think that in each orientation directions are assigned so that

---

[4]I believe that retinally disoriented written and printed words, pictures of faces, and the like are essentially uncorrectable, in the sense that they remain perceptually different from the way they look upright even after we have been able to identify them.

each orientation encountered leads to a different percept. Thus, an entire set of different memory traces is acquired, one for each orientation, and that is why recognition is later possible in any orientation. Although such a state of affairs could no doubt be created in an experiment with novel figures, it is doubtful if this occurs with multioriented objects in daily life. Rather, it would seem that an object such as a pair of scissors is orientation free, that is, no one region is taken as top, and so forth. After all, it is not only the case that we recognize a pair of scissors in any orientation, but that we perceive it as the *same shape* in any orientation. This suggests that we *can* abstract from orientation and focus entirely on the internal, intrafigural relationships. The ability to do so may itself be based upon a learning process.

### DIRECTION-OF-SCANNING THEORIES

If form perception required scanning the contour of the figure with the eyes, as once was believed necessary, then of course a change of orientation could lead to differences in sequence of scanning and, thus, to perceptual differences. This particular view is no longer held today as far as I know, but some investigators still consider direction of scanning relevant to the problem of orientation. In the case of reading, for example, we do tend to scan from left to right, and Kolers and Perkins have investigated the effect of this factor in orientational transformations of various kinds (Kolers, 1968; Kolers & Perkins, 1969a, b).[5] They have concluded that it *is* relevant, although not in the simple way one might predict. I would think that there are two factors here that must be unscrambled before the matter will be clear. Letter order is certainly crucial in decoding words, but letter order and temporal sequence of fixation are not one and the same. One can scan a word from right to left and easily recognize it because the spatially given left-to-right letter order remains unchanged.

Lila Ghent (1960, 1961, 1964) has demonstrated that young children perceive figures—even novel figures—as right side up only

[5]Kolers' and Perkins' work is described in detail in the Appendix (pages 150–154).

in certain orientations. She presents evidence that this judgment depends upon the focal part of the figure being in the upper portion, and speculates that children tend to scan figures from the top down. If the eye is drawn to the focal part of the figure and this is at the top, then scanning can proceed in the preferred way. If, however, the focal part is at the bottom, the child is forced to reverse his preferred direction of scanning, and that is why he considers figures in this orientation as upside down. In a separate paper (Ghent & Bernstein, 1961), it was shown that children's ability to match a tachistoscopically presented standard to a comparison figure is superior when the standard is "upright," where "upright" means the figure is in an orientation that children would judge to be upright. ("Upright" does not mean that the standard is in the same orientation as the matching comparison figure. This was found not to affect performance.) Presumably, if the focal part is at the bottom, the child tends to begin there, and then he can no longer follow his natural tendency to scan in a downward direction. Thus there is indirect evidence concerning the hypothesized direction of scanning, but not direct evidence based on recording or observing eye movement.

Ghent's interesting discovery seems to be relevant to the question of intrinsic orientation (see page 38), that is, factors within a figure that may determine its phenomenally perceived orientation. As far as I can make out, this finding is not intended to explain why the same figure acquires a different shape in different orientations, which is the question of primary interest in the present monograph. Of course, it is possible to argue that by virtue of the tendency to scan from top to bottom (assuming there to be such a tendency in adults as well as children), any change in orientation will affect the temporal sequence in which the parts of a figure are seen. In tachistoscopic presentation, it will affect which part of the figure is registered foveally. This in turn could be considered the basis of phenomenal change and loss of recognition. However, such a claim about scanning as a basis of perceived form no longer can be taken seriously. One can scan a figure in any direction without this having the slightest effect on its apparent shape, and one can perceive and recognize figures that do not subtend too large a visual angle in brief tachistoscopic exposures while fixating a central region.[6]

Hebb (1949) suggested a theory according to which the sequence of scanning movements by the eye was thought to play a role in the *development* of the perception of form. Thus, in the mature organism, forms are perceived without such scanning being necessary any longer. A change in the orientation of the image of a figure ought to lead to perceptual changes, according to Hebb's theory, because the proximal stimulus would be entirely different.

In addition to the arguments already made against any kind of theory of scanning as an explanation of the problem under investigation, the following observation can now be added. Such a theory would not do justice to the facts about orientation reported here, either under the category of "assignment of direction" factor or "retinal" factor. For example, a figure looks different if we misperceive where its top is even if its orientation with respect to the observer is unchanged. Presumably directions of scanning would be governed by the axis of the head. Furthermore, maximum change occurs for tilts of 45 or 90°, not 180°. As far as retinal change alone is concerned, most figures do not look different when there is no change in where the top is located. Yet direction of scanning would presumably be different.

These, then, are the kinds of explanations that have been put forth at one time or another to deal with the facts concerning orientation in form perception.

---

[6]Hochberg (1968) has presented convincing evidence that for figures extending over an appreciable visual angle, scanning is necessary for certainty about details of the figure that are not yet registered foveally. The percept that emerges is then the result of a "schematic map" integrating the successive views. However, the same percept would result regardless of direction of scanning.

Scanning can also be thought of as the serial processing of a figure by the perceptual system, rather than as sequential eye movements. Defined in this way, it is possible to try to account for perceptual change resulting from change of figural orientation as a function of changes in the order of processing of the parts of a figure, provided that there is a preferred direction for such scanning. But the fact is that the end result should be the same regardless of order of processing.

### Anisotropy and Form Perception

The fact that form is affected by orientation is sometimes said to illustrate the more general fact of anisotropy of visual space. Anisotropy is used here to mean that visual space has different properties in different directions. Perhaps the best example of such anisotropy is the vertical–horizontal illusion—the fact that a vertical line appears to be slightly longer than an objectively equal horizontal line. A possibly related fact is the tendency for the velocity of a vertically moving object to appear appreciably greater than that of a horizontally moving object of the same physical velocity (Brown, 1931). It is known that visual acuity is superior along vertical or horizontal directions compared with oblique directions. Judgment of angle size is also believed to be a function of orientation, and the greater sensitivity to judgment of right angles when the sides are horizontal and vertical has been noted earlier.

Whether or not it adds anything to our knowledge to subsume all facts of this kind under the heading of an impressive-sounding term like anisotropy is questionable, particularly if it proves to be the case that each phenomenon requires a different explanation. In any case, it would seem misleading to think of form changes induced by changes in orientation as exemplifying anisotropy. If forms looked different solely as a result of changes in the orientation of their retinal image and its cortical representation, and if, in turn, such perceptual effects resulted from differences in the neural substrate as a function of direction, then anisotropy would seem to be an appropriate term to describe such effects. In our laboratory, we have found that the vertical–horizontal illusion is based on retinal coordinates rather than the perceived vertical–horizontal coordinates, because the extent perceived to be longest is always the one parallel to the sagittal axis of the head, regardless of the way the head is oriented in space.[7] Others have obtained the same result (Künnapas, 1958; Morinaga, Noguchi, & Ohishi, 1962). If this

---

[7] Unpublished research conducted by the author and Janet Simon.

means that, for reasons as yet unknown, a vertically oriented cortical representation gives rise to a greater phenomenal extent than an objectively equal horizontally oriented cortical representation, then the vertical–horizontal illusion is based on anisotropy of the neural substrate. Presumably, then, the orientation of any figure's image in the substrate would reflect that anisotropy.

The vertical–horizontal illusion is a modest one, however—of the order of a 6–8% difference in perceived length. The changes in perceived form that are, therefore, reducible to a manifestation of such underlying anisotropy would also be modest and, in point of fact, are barely noticeable. When experiments are performed to isolate the retinal factor, such as viewing an upright figure from a tilted body position, there is generally *no* discernible effect of the retinal change and *no* decline in recognition. There is an effect of retinal orientation in the case of material such as word figures, but why should the anisotropy of the substrate only make itself felt for such stimulus material? Furthermore, the vertical–horizontal anisotropy would disappear for orientation changes of 180°, which is precisely the one that leads to a maximum change in such material.

The major factor affecting perceived form is the assignment of directions. With no change in the orientation of the retinal image and its cortical representation and even with no change in the objective orientation of a figure in space, a figure can be made to appear entirely different by the expedient of altering its up–down, left–right phenomenal axes. This can be accomplished by instructions or experimental set. Should this be thought of as anisotropy? To be sure, the perceived vertical axis of a figure is phenomenally different from the perceived horizontal axis; and the "bottom" of a figure is phenomenally different from the "top," and so forth. Furthermore, it is true that phenomenal space has up–down, left–right coordinates and that therefore this space is not homogenous in all directions. But in the example under discussion, the perceived vertical axis of the figure is not aligned with the perceived vertical axis of space. Hence, it is not a change of the figure's orientation with respect to the perceived vertical and horizontal axes of space that matters, but the more circumscribed assignment of directions to the figure per se. Indeed, with the proper assignment of directions, a physically tilted figure will look exactly the way it does when upright. So, to speak of anisotropy here seems inappropriate.

## Retinal Change and
## Change of Assigned Directions Combined

Having isolated two factors by appropriate experimental techniques, the question arises as to how to understand the effect of simultaneous change in the retinal orientation and assigned directions of a figure. Do the effects of the two factors combine in some way?

The answer, I believe, is that either one or the other factor can be at work, but not both together. If a figure is tilted into a new orientation, and the observer, not knowing this, assigns directions to it on the basis of environmental cues, he will probably not recognize it. This would be explicable in terms of the "assignment of directions" factor. Therefore, by definition, no attempt to correct for change of orientation is taking place.

Only if the observer has correct information concerning the location of the top and bottom of the figure can he enter into the correction process that is the essence of the retinal factor. Therefore, no additional disturbance should ensue from the retinal change per se. The decline in recognition should be the same for an environmentally tilted figure (not known to be tilted) whether the observer remains upright or is tilted by the same amount as the figure.

Conversely, if the observer knows that the figure is tilted, and if he knows where its top is located, then only the retinal factor entailing correction is relevant. By definition, the assignment of directions factor cannot enter in.

If this reasoning is correct, that only one or the other factor can play a role in any given case, it would seem to follow that the techniques employed here to isolate the two factors were not absolutely essential. To isolate the assignment of directions factor, both observer and figure were tilted by the same amount (pages 26–34). It now seems clear that this factor can be isolated just as effectively by tilting only the figure, provided steps are taken to ensure that the observer is unaware of this fact. Therefore, the effect of degree of disorientation on phenomenal appearance can be studied simply by presenting the test figure in various orientations from 0 to 180°, keeping the training figure and the observer always upright. (This technique may even eliminate some of the difficulties with the experiment we did perform (see the Appendix, pages 138–139).

Since this is essentially the method used by Dearborn (1899), and since his method was similar in other respects to the one we employed, it is of interest to consider his findings in detail. In Dearborn's study, a series of novel inkblot figures was presented, the figures appearing again later in the series in either unchanged orientation or tilted 90° clockwise or counterclockwise, rotated 180°, left–right reversed, or inverted. Recognition fell off for each of the changed orientations. The percentages of correct recognitions were as follows: 0°, 70%; 90° clockwise, 43%; 90° counterclockwise, 33%; 180°, 51%; left–right reversed, 46%; inverted, 32%. New figures were incorrectly "recognized" 30% of the time. However, of Dearborn's nine observers, two incorrectly identified such a high percentage of *new* figures as to cast doubt on the meaning of their responses to previously seen figures. Eliminating them and recomputing the averages for the remaining seven observers give the results shown in Table 5. The average amount of new figures falsely identified for these observers was 22%.

The trend of the results is remarkably similar to that found in our study, in which change of 90° proved most disturbing. (In Dearborn's experiment, the fact that the average of the two 90° conditions is roughly 24% is close to signifying no recognition,

**TABLE 5**

Dearborn's Experiment: Mean Percentage Recognized for Seven Observers

| Orientation of test figure | 0 | 90° clockwise | 90° counterclockwise | 180° | Inverted | Left–right reversed |
|---|---|---|---|---|---|---|
| Mean % | 60 | 28 | 20 | 44.5 | 35.5 | 47 |

since 22% of *new* figures are falsely recognized.) The left–right reversal change proved least disturbing, and the 180° rotation far less disturbing than 90° tilt (see Table 1, page 32). Comparison of absolute level of performance across the two experiments is not appropriate, since the conditions were quite different.

As to the technique used to isolate the retinal factor, namely, requiring a tilted observer to view an environmentally upright figure, this too is not absolutely necessary. In principle, the correction process can be studied as well when the observer remains upright and views a disoriented figure, as long as he is informed about the nature of the disorientation. However, it is unlikely that information of this kind, amounting essentially to knowledge about directions, influences the correction process as effectively as direct perceptual cues like gravity and the visual frame of reference. We have found that the reaction time needed to identify inverted letters viewed by an upright observer is greater than that needed to identify upright letters viewed by an inverted observer, even though the observer knows about the orientation of the letters in both cases.[8] Therefore, the technique of having the figure upright and the observer tilted is recommended as the method for studying the correction process under optimum conditions.[9]

[8]Unpublished research conducted by the author and Charles Bebber.

[9]In considering factors that determine the directions assigned to figures, I had earlier (pages 21–22) included a mental set supplied by information given by instructions. Such a set was shown to exert a powerful influence on perceived shape. When the orientation suggested by the instructions is congruent with that given by the egocentric coordinates—for example, the observer is tilted 90° clockwise and

## The "Purpose" of Change of Appearance in Form with Change of Orientation

One might well ask what "purpose" is served by the fact that orientation alters the appearance of forms. There clearly are disadvantages. Were it not for an effect of orientation on perceived shape, it would not be necessary to correct a figure whenever we viewed it from a different posture. Shape would simply be a function of the internal geometry of a figure, so that it would look the same regardless of how its image fell on the retina. And by the same token, there would be no instance of failure of correction, as there is with certain material. Also, if a figure seen previously were encountered again when *it* was in a new orientation, recognition would not fail, as in point of fact it often does.

Against these disadvantages is the increase in efficiency of representation of different objects. With direction entering into perceived form, the same internal geometry can represent a number of discriminably different shapes. For example, a straight line with a loop at one end can represent four letters of the alphabet, only because direction enters into the perception. Also, objects or figures which in point of fact do differ somewhat in their internal geometries would otherwise appear far more similar to one another than they now do. For example, the two figures in Fig. 63 look quite different. If, however, perceived orientations played *no* role in such appearance, if only the internal geometry mattered, then they would look quite similar. Thus by tilting Fig. 63b about 120°

---

is told the top of the figure is in this same direction—there is no difficulty at all. Without these instructions, the top would be located differently and the figure would look quite different. However, such a set can be effective even if the suggested orientation is not congruent with egocentric directionalization (page 22). In that event, the effectiveness of instructions depends upon correction. If the figure is not too difficult and/or the angular difference between egocentric orientation and that determined by instructions is not too large, information of this kind can be very effective. Otherwise, as noted above, information of this kind is not as effective as that of a direct sensory nature.

(a)                                 (b)

**FIG. 63**

**FIG. 64**

clockwise (Fig. 64), it now appears to be quite similar to Fig. 63a. Thus, there would be a good deal more confusing of objects and figures with one another than there is now.

Since in nature (and in environments constructed by men), immovable objects do have one orientation, and many living things that do move tend to maintain one orientation, direction within objects can contribute to the way they look with relative impunity, as long as a correction process operates when the *observer's* orientation is altered. Apparently the evolutionary "cost" of acquiring the correction mechanism was offset by the gain in efficiency of form discrimination. The difficulty of correction with material as complex as words was not something the evolutionary mechanism could have anticipated. It is well known that those processes that generally lead to veridical perception also occasionally lead to illusion and misperception.

## The Issue of Adaptation
## to a Disoriented Retinal Image

The existence of retinally determined egocentric coordinates is at the very heart of the issue raised by Stratton's (1896, 1897a,

b) famous experiment on inversion of the retinal image by lenses. It is clear that this experiment is concerned with egocentric orientation when it is realized that an observer wearing such a system of lenses suffers from the same inversion experiences whether he is viewing objects in a vertical plane from an upright position, or whether he is viewing objects in a horizontal plane—for example, as in bending over and viewing the ground. In fact, were it not for the existence of an egocentric sense of up–down and left–right tied to retinal coordinates, it would be hard to understand why the world would look inverted at all, even at the outset of the experiment.

What is interesting about experiments of this kind in connection with the problem under discussion is that the evidence suggests that perceptual adaptation to the inverted image is very difficult to achieve and, in fact, may not occur at all. (I am distinguishing perceptual adaptation, by which I mean whether things look upside down or right side up, from visual–motor coordination. The latter kind of adaptation does occur, without any doubt.) Even perceptual adaptation to lesser degrees of prismatic tilting of the retinal image, rather than inversion, is slight (Mack & Rock, 1968).[10] This would seem to mean that there is a deeply ingrained tendency to "project" egocentric up–down, left–right coordinates onto the scene, as determined by the corresponding retinal coordinates. In other words, it is very difficult to effect any change in the egocentric directions signified by stimulation of specific retinal orientations. Yet it is this very tendency to perceive these directions with the consequence of imbuing a figure with an egocentric top, bottom, and

[10]Other experiments on exposure to a prismatically tilted image have been performed with a fair degree of adaptation obtained within an hour or two. See Mikaelian and Held (1964), and Ebenholtz (1966). In these experiments, no attempt was made to distinguish perceived egocentric orientation from perceived environmental orientation. If, however, the change that occurs can be assumed to be in egocentric orientation signified by a specific retinal orientation, and if it is true that little or no adaptation occurs in the case of exposure to an *inverted* image, then one might be tempted to relate this difference to the greater difficulty in correcting figures that are rotated 180° as compared to lesser degrees of disorientation.

sides that must be overcome in the process of correcting for retinally disoriented forms.

In considering the matter of possible adaptation to optical inversion of the retinal image, the question of the origin of perceived egocentric orientation naturally arises. The difficulty in achieving adaptation in human beings, and the finding that the visual–motor coordination of salamanders is irrevocably disrupted by inversion of the eye, points toward a possible innate basis of such perception (Sperry, 1943; Stone, 1944). On the other hand, logical considerations suggest that egocentric orientation is learned, at least in human beings. What we mean by "egocentric orientation" is how an object appears to be oriented with respect to the head (or body), or which direction along that object appears to be "up," that is, in the chin-to-forehead direction, or "down," that is, in the forehead-to-chin direction, and so forth.[11] Thus, the very meaning of the perception in question is tied to mental contents concerning the body as an object in awareness. It does not seem plausible to believe that this is innately given. Rather, it is plausible to think it is learned on the basis of movement and other kinds of information.[12] If learned, the evidence considered here on adaptation and on the perception of retinally disoriented figures suggests an association of such strength and permanence as to approach irreversibility.

There are a few observations which seem to suggest some relation-

[11]Whether or not one will consider a figure seen in a horizontal plane to be upright may depend on how it is orientated with respect to the entire body rather than only the head. When the head is not aligned with the rest of the body, Begelman (1968) has shown that a figure placed near the feet will be judged upright on the basis of how it is oriented to the body rather than to the head. It makes sense that the body would be taken as the frame of reference for directionalization under such circumstances, but I would think this process entails correcting for retinal orientation by taking into account head orientation, just as when a tilted observer views an environmentally upright object. That retinal orientation is directly tied to perceived egocentric orientation at a primitive level, prior to any such correction process, is evidenced by the fact that if Begelman's experiment were done with material such as words or faces, recognition would be more difficult in any orientation but the retinally normal one.

[12]For a discussion of the work on adaptation to a disoriented image and the related issues referred to above, see Rock (1966, Chapter 2).

ship between adaptation and the perceived orientation of figures. A number of investigators, including Stratton, have noted that the initial difficulty in recognizing various objects and figures seen through lenses or prisms disappeared in the course of their study. This fact has no necessary bearing on adaptation to the altered orientation. It simply means that the observer became increasingly familiar with the figures in their new orientation—for example, inverted word figures. Of course, if perceptual adaptation to the new retinal orientation actually occurred, then presumably figures never even seen during prior prism exposure would be immediately recognized in their new retinal orientation, and they would appear to be upright.

An effect that has been likened to adaptation is the tendency to be unaware of the difference in size between the upper and lower halves of certain familiar figures, such as a typeface S or 8. When these are seen upside down, it is immediately apparent that the lower halves are smaller. Yet right side up it was not apparent that the upper halves were smaller. This would seem to be a matter of becoming accustomed to a certain percept, because with attention directed to it, we are perfectly capable of noting the size difference in the upright figures. Upside down, the size difference obtrudes on us because it is the opposite of the one to which we have grown accustomed.

So, to sum up, the problem of adaptation to a disoriented image and the problem of the perception of disoriented figures are related, in that they both are a function of the existence of retinally determined egocentric coordinates. Both the difficulty of adaptation to a rotated image and the necessity and difficulty of correcting egocentrically tilted figures stem from the association between fixed retinal directions and the egocentric direction. Either this association is innately determined, or it is learned early in life to a strength which is virtually irreversible. Observations made by Stratton and others concerning adaptation to objects that initially appear strange and unrecognizable probably signify little more than a process of growing accustomed to such objects in their new orientation.

## Form Orientation in Children

It has been claimed that, unlike adults, young children are indifferent to the orientation of figures. This belief seems to have its origin in the fact that young children are unconcerned with the orientation of pictures, so that they are as likely to view a page upside down or tilted as upright, and yet recognize the object pictured. They also are likely to draw objects in varying orientations. Some experimental studies have been interpreted as supporting these observations.

In well-designed laboratory tests of this question, however, it has been found that young children do have more difficulty in recognizing rotated figures than figures which remain upright (Ghent, 1960; Brooks & Goldstein, 1963; Pappalardo, 1966; Rock, 1952; see Howard & Templeton, 1966, for a review of the literature). In fact, compared with adults, several studies showed that they have *more* difficulty in recognizing rotated figures. Furthermore, when they are required to learn to discriminate between a figure in its upright and rotated form, they can do so as easily as for two geometrically different figures, unless the rotated figure is a left–right reversal (Rudel & Teuber, 1963). If they were indifferent to orientation, it would be impossible to make such discriminations.

The case of left–right reversal should be considered separately, because adults too often confuse such reversals with the original figure. Left–right reversals do look very much like the originals. The probable explanation of this fact has already been discussed. That adults *do* discriminate cases of reversal from nonreversal while young children do not is no doubt the result of much overlearning of the material—for example letters—or of the capacity of adults to use verbal mnemonics concerning left and right.

For other kinds of orientation change, however, the facts derived from laboratory experiments seem to contradict the widespread belief that young children are indifferent to orientation. How can these findings be reconciled with the more casual observations of children in the home and school? To consider one kind of observation, children confuse the letters *p, d, b,* and *q* when they are first learning to read more often than they confuse other letters with one another. Of course, *q* is a left–right reversal of *p,* and *d* of *b,* so these confusions are understandable. As for confusing *p* and *q* with either *b* or *d,* one might speculate that they too look very similar: They each contain a vertical line with a loop at one end.

The findings of one laboratory study might be considered to support the assumption that young children are indifferent to orientation (Gibson, Gibson, Pick, & Osser, 1962). Children of various ages were required to indicate which among many transformations of a simple standard figure were "exactly like" the standard. Some of the transformations were of orientation, while others were not. The youngest children had particular difficulty with the orientational transformation, that is, they often erred by calling them the same as the standard.

But it is unlikely, in this experiment, that the *older* children made correct identifications because they failed to recognize the rotated figures. Only if that were true might the errors of the younger children imply, by comparison, no effect of orientation on phenomenal shape. The procedure of the experiment entailed the comparison of the standard figure with a simultaneously presented row of transformations of it. Thus, the child no doubt perceives all the transformations as similar to the standard, and his task becomes one of deciding which are and which are not "exactly like" it. Therefore, when the older child says "no" to the rotated figures, it is not because he perceives these as phenomenally different shapes (although he might do so, as would an adult in a differently designed experiment where special pains are taken to ensure incorrect assignment of directions to the test figures), but rather because he understands he should say "no" because the orientation does not match that of the standard. The "no" response is based on the conscious realization that, while the figure may look the same, it is in a different orientation, and that if a figure is in a different orientation it is not "exactly the same" as the standard. In other words, the instructions require abstracting the fact of orientation difference per se. It is very probable that, when orientation of form is in question, young children differ in at least one respect from older ones and from adults—namely, they are less inclined to notice or to think about the figure's orientation or to consider it worth mentioning. Therefore, in this experiment, their failure to do so results in errors.[13] Consequently this experiment is not germane to the question at issue here—namely, is phenomenal shape unaffected by orientation for young children?

Before one can hope to understand the developmental aspect of a psychological function, it is necessary to be clear about the nature of that function in the adult. We now know that there are two distinct effects of change of orientation on form perception in the adult, and one of these is the result of a change in the assignment of directions. So the question here is whether or not a figure looks different to young children when different regions are at the top, bottom, and sides. Before it can be expected that figural orientation would make a difference to a child, it must be assumed that directions such as "top" and "bottom" are discriminated and, furthermore, that figures are perceived in terms of these directions. Once the infant begins to walk, it would seem safe to assume that "up" and "down" are distinguished from one another, so that if a figure is seen in a vertical plane, the child is at least capable of perceiving it in terms of "top" and "bottom." If the child does perceive a figure in terms of which region is its top and which its bottom, this would lead to form perceptions similar to those of an adult. That being the case, a shift of assigned

[13]There are several other experiments in the literature which point to just this fact. See, for example, an experiment by Rice (1930).

In addition to the problem raised here about the meaning of "yes" and "no" responses, or "same" and "different" responses in young children, there are several other questions of method which warrant attention in studies of this kind. One is the inadvisability of testing by brief tachistoscopic exposure with young children because, as Ghent has suggested, they may scan in a specific direction. Another is the question of absolute level of performance. It may be desirable to permit the youngest children to have more time or more exposure to the figures in training than older children or adults, since otherwise their absolute level of recognition will be substantially lower.

directions for most figures should lead to a change in perceptions for children as well as for adults. As noted, the evidence available seems to bear this out.

What might we expect to be the case for children when there is only retinal change? Are there grounds for expecting that children would have less difficulty than adults in recognizing figures whose assigned directions are *not* changed but which are not retinally upright? Only if egocentric directions come about as the result of past experience might one think that the very young child does not yet have an egocentric "up," "down," "left," or "right." If so, the very young child should not be troubled by changes in the orientation of the retinal image, since there would be no need to suppress an egocentrically determined percept, and thus no problem in perceiving in accordance with assigned directions wherever they happened to fall retinally. However, if the child does have egocentric coordinates in no way different from the adult, one would imagine he would have *more*, not less, difficulty in recognizing retinally disoriented material such as faces. This statement is based upon the theoretical analysis presented earlier, that the difficulty here is the necessity of visualizing how something would look were it egocentrically upright. Such a cognitive task should, if anything, be more difficult for a child.

There is one experiment that attempted to determine whether young children assign directions to figures solely in terms of egocentric coordinates (Pappalardo, 1966). The children were required to view figures projected onto a horizontal plane—the ceiling—from a reclining position. In that plane, figural direction can be determined only by egocentric coordinates. The nonsense figures were first shown in one orientation, then once again either in that same orientation or an altered one. The children were to say whether the figures in the test were the same as those shown previously. Five- and 10-year-olds and adults recognized more egocentrically upright figures than disoriented figures. In fact, the superiority in recognition of upright over disoriented figures was greater the *younger* the age group, although this trend fell short of significance.

The results thus demonstrate that presentation of figures in a horizontal plane does not reduce or eliminate an effect of orientation
on recognition in young children. Whether innately determined
or learned, 5-year-old children do assign directions on the basis
of egocentric coordinates. As a result, change of figural orientation
leads to change of assigned directions and, hence, to poorer recognition.[14]

A recent well-designed experiment directly tested the question
of whether young children are indifferent to orientation with material known to disturb recognition in adults (Brooks & Goldstein,
1963). The task for the children was to identify inverted photographs of their classmates that the week before they succeeded
in identifying right side up. Since it was clear that they were looking
at inverted faces, the experiment was concerned with the retinal
factor, with the ability to correct for the abnormal egocentric orientation of the test material. Only pictures correctly identified the
week before were shown, and the score was the percentage of
those now recognized upside down. There was no time restriction.
The pictures were doctored to eliminate features that might lead
to easy identification, such as the hair, ears, and clothing. Children
from 3 to 14 years old were tested. The results showed that recognition of the inverted pictures increased with age, from roughly 60
to 70% for 3- to 4-year-olds to 90 to 100% for 10- to 14-year-olds.
Therefore, it would seem that young children have more difficulty
correcting than older children.[15]

To sum up, then, it would seem probable that a change in assignment of directions to figures produces the same phenomenal

[14]In this study, the more traditional method of presenting upright and rotated
figures on a vertical screen was also employed. It was found that upright test figures
were recognized by young children more frequently than rotated test figures, and
the difference was even greater than for adults.

[15]In a later, as yet unpublished, study, Goldstein included high school and college
age subjects as well as more young children but none in the 3–4-year-old age group.
Here the trend seems to reverse itself. The adults identified proportionately *fewer*
inverted pictures of previously identified upright pictures than did the 10–14-year-
old children. For the *combined* data of the two studies, the very young children and
the college students have the most difficulty with the inverted faces.

change for children as it does for adults. Also, a change from the customary upright retinal orientation of certain kinds of material leads to the same difficulty of correction, if not more so, that adults experience.

It is therefore possible that what has been universally observed about the indifference to orientation among preschool children when they look at or draw pictures is not that form and recognition of form is unaffected by orientation, but rather that orientation per se is not noticed or attended to. Since children can recognize on the basis of many features and details, they are indifferent to the way a picture is oriented. They have not yet learned that it is customary and desirable to orient a picture in only one way and they do not realize that a particular orientation might improve their recognition.[16]

[16]Infants as young as six months of age apparently can discriminate among various orientations of the same form although orientation is not a salient dimension for them (McGurk, 1970, 1972a, b).

★
★  ★

CHAPTER VI

# Implications for a
# Theory of Form Perception

I have suggested that the reason why a change in the directions assigned to a figure affects its phenomenal shape is that it leads to a different cognitive description of the figure. Examples have been given of what is meant by this. When the orientation of the figure is unchanged and the observer views it from an altered posture, recognition generally succeeds because the figural description is essentially the same. I have argued that under these circumstances it is necessary to correct for the novel orientation of the retinal image, and that this process entails an act of visualization. That is, the observer must imagine how the figure would look if its up–down, left–right axes were aligned with his egocentric axes before he can properly describe the figure. Thus, the perceptual process in the case of form includes certain cognitive events such as description and visualization. This points to a theory that

113

is rather different from the ones that are current among sensory physiologists based exclusively on the physical characteristics of the impinging form stimulus.

How does one relate this aspect of form perception to other aspects that have nothing to do with orientation? After all, certain features of every figure must affect the way it looks quite apart from orientation, as for example, whether it is elongated or compact, curvilinear or rectilinear, open or closed, and so forth. Furthermore, there are cases where orientation does not seem to affect phenomenal shape at all, as in figures that may be thought of as orientation free (scissors, pipes, and the like).

There are two ways of dealing with the hypothesis of description based on figural orientation:

1. Such a description is supplemental to other, entirely different, kinds of mechanisms that determine form perception.
2. Form perception in general is the result of cognitive description.

According to 1, form is first determined by mechanisms that are presumed to underlie contour formation and perceptual organization. At this point, those aspects of the figure are determined by the process of description that takes account of orientation, and are added to the already existing form. According to 2, perceived form is entirely the result of a process of description.

For a variety of reasons, I believe the second hypothesis to be the correct one. First of all, it is unparsimonious to believe that entirely different mechanisms are at work, some to determine the nonorientational aspect of form and others to determine the orientational aspect. It is plausible to think that phenomenal form results from a process of description that includes features governed by assigned directions and features not so governed. The process of description is simultaneously determined by both the internal geometry of the figure and by the effect of the directions assigned to it. Where orientation does not affect phenomenal shape, we can assume that the process of description does not concern itself with direction, but only with the internal geometry.

In the last century and earlier, it was customary to regard form perception as a derivative of the perceived locations of all the points making it up. For a number of reasons, this way of looking at form perception is rarely if ever considered anymore. The Gestalt critique of elementarism and its emphasis on whole qualities is one such reason. Another is the emphasis that has been placed on the perception of contours by contemporary investigators, and on the search for the mechanisms that underlie contour formation. [Hebb's cell assemblies; Marshall and Talbot's peak of the distribution of cortical excitation (1942); Hubel and Wiesel's orientation-specific detectors; Köhler and Wallach's (1944) direct current fields, and the like]. In my opinion, this emphasis on contour perception and the implicit assumption that it is more or less equivalent to form perception mistakes the building blocks for the building itself. Contours are simply markers of the location of the boundaries of a figure.

In point of fact, contours are not necessary for form perception. Just as the location of a single point is perceived, so the location of several points is perceived and, in the latter case, one is aware of the location of these points with respect to one another. This is the essence of form perception. Several dot figures are shown in Fig. 65, whose overall shapes are simply a function of the location of the points with respect to one another.

Even more to the point is the phenomenon of subjective contour. Under certain conditions, we perceive contours where none exist physically. Figure 66 is an example. The exact conditions which lead to subjective contour and the mechanism underlying it are still under investigation. However, it seems quite likely that it results from a process of imagining a contour to be present because the stimulus array can be interpreted most plausibly as a surface of a

FIG. 65

**FIG. 66**

given shape lying over certain components of the array. This phenomenon illustrates that perceived forms should not be thought of as deriving from a set of contours since here the contour is not only absent as a stimulus but it only becomes a psychological reality at the moment the form as a whole is imagined.

A single moving point will be perceived as describing a path that has a particular shape. This is true even if the observer is instructed to track the point with his eyes, the point being luminous and presented in the dark. Under these conditions, the image of the point remains in one region of the retina. Because the changing direction of the eyes provides information about the changing location of the point, the observer is able to perceive the various locations of the point with respect to one another. Such a set of relative locations, it is being argued here, is what is essential for form perception. Furthermore, if in tracking a moving point a stationary point is introduced, an observer has no impression of the path of the second, stationary point, despite the fact that the image of this second point describes a path over the retina. The perceived location of this second point is constant (position constancy), so that here one cannot speak of a set of locations of the point which differ with respect to one another. Hence, there can be no perception of a path of a given shape.

The impression that one is viewing an *extended figure*, rather than a point describing a path, is obtained if a narrow slit, which reveals only a small segment of a figure at a time, is moved back and forth in front of a figure. Since here too the impression of a line figure occurs even with the tracking of the slit, this effect can be considered to be a demonstration of form perception without a retinal image (Rock & Halper, 1969). Certainly it demonstrates perception of a form with phenomenal contours, without any contours being physically present. There appear to be other cognitive factors at work here, because the impression of a line figure occurs only if the observer has the impression that he is looking through a slit at something revealed behind it.

Recently, Julesz (1971) has demonstrated that it is possible to perceive forms on the basis of binocular disparities between retinal images, which themselves contain no discernible forms. Each eye is separately presented with a random pattern of light and dark spots. The same pattern is shown to each eye, except for a given region of one pattern that is displaced slightly with respect to the rest. As a result of the binocular disparity thereby created, a form is perceived standing out in depth from the rest of the pattern. This discovery has been looked upon in terms of its relevance to the problem of depth perception, but it is also significant with regard to the problem of form perception. It seems to me that a form is perceived because the binocular disparities serve to mark *a set of locations in the field,* namely, those that are disparate, despite the fact that no image of the form per se and no contours of the form exist in either eye. It is true that there are miniature contours, so to speak, present in each retinal image: the small clusterings of spots that can be said to produce subsets of forms. No doubt it is the disparities between these clusterings that yield the form in depth. However, the *binocular* form that is perceived has a phenomenal contour that is not the sum of any of these clusterings, since no such overall contour is perceived with either eye alone. Therefore, it seems correct to say that the set of disparate clusterings are markers of locations which determine the binocular form.

On the basis of what has been said above, one can maintain

that phenomenal form is the end result of detecting how a set of points are located with respect to one another. One can accept this conclusion without necessarily drawing any further conclusions from it about cognitive description. Also, one could argue that, given such a set of relative locations, a synthesis occurs—the precise mechanism of which is unknown—and this synthesis results in a particular phenomenal shape.[1] However, I am suggesting that this synthesis is essentially an act of description that is based in large measure on such relative locations (and needless to say is also based on the assignment of directions to the array as a whole). A theory according to which form is a derivative of a set of perceived locations is quite compatible with the notion of the description of an array of such locations as the basis of phenomenal shape.

While there is as yet no decisive evidence in support of this theory—other than perhaps what is presented in this mono-graph—there are a number of facts about form perception that can be understood in these terms. Consider, for example, the prob-lem of perceiving extremely complex figures. As noted earlier, there is reason to believe that not every nuance of such a figure is perceived on an initial encounter, although the figure as a whole is clearly imaged on the retina. The basis for this statement is the fact that without considerable experience with such figures, one is generally unable to differentiate them from other similar figures seen at a later time. This would make sense if it is assumed that the process of description at the time of the original encounter is limited to the overall shape quality. If, instead, form perception is a process not unlike photographic registration, it would be hard

---

[1]There is the problem of perceptual organization to be taken into account. Some mechanism must be responsible for the fact that all the points constituting the figure, and only those points, are grouped together as one entity distinct from background and other entities in the field. But such groupings cannot be the basis of synthesis referred to above, because by synthesis is meant here the collective apprehension of all the locations of points constituting a form such that its overall shape is perceived. In other words, it is not grouping which makes one collection of points different in shape from another, but the specific geometry of the set as a whole.

to understand why complexity should have any bearing at all on what is perceived and, therefore, what can be remembered.

A related fact is that attention is of some importance in form perception. We have been able to demonstrate in our laboratory that if conditions are such that an observer is not paying attention to a figure, although he is looking directly at it for an adequate duration of time, he apparently does not perceive it the way he would if he had been paying attention to it.[2] Following such an exposure, far fewer observers are able to pick out the figure seen from among an array of alternatives presented immediately afterward than when they were paying attention to the figure. If nothing of a cognitive nature is involved in form perception, it is difficult to see why attention should be relevant. It seems unlikely that the visual signals arising from each part of the figure do not reach the visual cortex as a result of inattention.

The facts of transposition are quite compatible with the theory of cognitive description. In the half century that has elapsed since the Gestalt psychologists have forcefully called these facts to our attention, there still is no adequate explanation of the basis for transposition, If, however, form perception results from description based on internal geometry and figural orientation, then it would follow that figures transposed in size, position, and even retinal orientation would appear to be the same shape.

The transposability of forms across the visual and tactual modalities is perhaps an even more impressive fact. What remains the same so that a previously seen figure can now be recognized by touch, or vice versa? The factor that remains the same is clearly the shape that is apprehended, but in what medium can that apprehension be taking place in such a way that there is an equivalence across modalities? The answer could well be a transsensory or cognitive medium. The finding reported in Chapter III of an effect of disorientation on the recognition of *tactually* experienced shape can perhaps best be explained along similar lines.

[2]An unpublished study conducted by the author and F. Halper.

The constancy of perceived shape when a figure is in a plane sloped or slanted with respect to the frontal plane (Fig. 1b and c, Chapter I, page 2) implies a process of taking into account the slope or slant of the figure. It thus makes sense to suggest that the end result of such a process is a description of the figure in terms of its perceived geometry, rather than in terms of the geometry of its retinal image. For example, a circle at a slant would be described as a "round shape whose vertical and horizontal axes were *equal*."

I have implied that there are two aspects of a figure which determine how it will be described, namely, its internal geometry and the directions assigned to it. There are, however, other factors which have been pointed out by Goldmeier (1937) in his study of the basis of similarity in form perception. For example, most observers consider that Fig. 67b is more like Fig. 67a, the standard, than is Fig. 67c. Yet compared to Fig. 67a there is as much change in Fig. 67b as in c. Both entail the displacement of inner lines. Apparently b appears more similar because in Fig. 67a the two inner lines are grouped with one another as a pair, and Fig. 67b preserves this grouping, whereas Fig. 67c does not. The absolute distance of the pair from the upper part of the figure is of less importance. This kind of effect suggests—to the writer at least—that the process of description takes into account organizational factors.

Another example is shown in Fig. 68. Here most observers consider Fig. 68c to be more like the standard Fig. 68a than 68b.

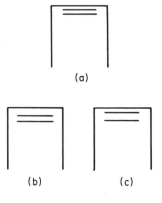

**FIG. 67**

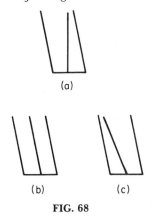

(a)

(b)          (c)

**FIG. 68**

Yet as far as absolute physical change is concerned, Fig. 68b is closer than Fig. 68c in similarity to Fig. 68a because the central line is displaced less than in Fig. 68c. But since both Fig. 68a and c would be described as "oblique open rectangles with tilted lines inside," they appear similar to one another. Figure 68b would have to be described as "a rectangle with a line parallel to the sides." This example suggests that the description is in part a function of the presence or absence of certain salient features, such as a tilted line or a parallel line. A more specific description, for instance, "a center line tilted by such an angle counterclockwise" may also occur, but still not play as important a role as the more general description.

## Implications for the Process of Recognition

Logically, recognition implies a relating of a present perception to prior memory. Assuming that memories endure in the form of traces and bearing in mind that only relating the percept to the appropriate trace (the trace of the object now being perceived) can lead to recognition, the problem becomes one of explaining the mechanism whereby the appropriate trace is selected from the vast number of different traces that exist. The similarity of the trace to the percept accounts for the selection. Either all traces are first scanned or searched, in which case the search ends when a trace that is similar to the percept is found, *or* the appropriate trace is aroused on the basis of similarity to the percept without search. In either case, it is the unconscious judgment of similarity that constitutes recognition.

But, we may ask what constitutes similarity? There may well be different answers to this question, depending upon the percept under consideration. Similarity of a sense quality such as color or odor may lead to recognition. In the case of form, although we are far from understanding the basis of form perception, we can say a few things about the basis for similarity. We know that the geometrical relationships among figural parts are crucial, since forms that are transposed in size and retinal position appear to be essentially the same forms. We also know, from Goldmeier's work, about the importance of effects of grouping, salient features, and the like.

Our findings here indicate that in addition to these internal geometrical relationships and other features of a figure, a factor external to the figure itself, namely, directionality, enters into the process of form perception. It was suggested that the orientation of the figure relative to the up–down, left–right axes imposed on the figure leads to a certain description, unconscious and nonverbal, of the shape. The description takes into account the internal features as well as directionality. Apparently then, this description forms the basis for the judgment of similarity that constitutes recognition. It is worth repeating that a figure whose orientation is changed from training to test will probably not be recognized, even if conditions are such that the image of the figure falls in the identical locus and orientation on the retina that it had in training. This shows the inadequacy of what has been called a template theory of recognition (Neisser, 1966). I am suggesting that recognition fails because the description of the figure in its new orientation is thoroughly different. Conversely, recognition generally succeeds even when the orientation of the figure's image changes, provided there is no change in the directions assigned to it. Here the description entails a process of correction based on taking into account one's own position and also carrying out a process of visualization, but as long as correction occurs, recognition will occur. Therefore, it would seem that the similarity of perceived form, which is the basis for recognition in such cases, is itself the end result of certain cognitive processes.

That recognition often fails in the case of retinally disoriented material like words or faces suggests certain limitations of the correction process. Apparently a multiplicity of figures or figure relationships within a single complex entity cannot all simultaneously be visualized in a different orientation from the one they are in. Thus the necessary correct description is not achieved for all components, and therefore correct recognition cannot occur. It is interesting to realize that when the same complex stimulus, such as a long word, *is* phenomenally and retinally upright, recognition is possible. Although no corrective visualizing is then necessary, presumably a figural description of all or most of the component letters is necessary, entailing reference to their up–down, left–right axes. No doubt the vast experience we have in looking at figure complexes such as words enables us to recognize them at a glance, but nevertheless such recognition implies that various component letters are perceived. And perception of these various letter forms in turn implies that many more than one of them can be "described" at the same time.

★

★  ★

CHAPTER VII

# Summary and Conclusions

When the orientation of a figure in a frontal plane is changed it will generally look different and, as a result, will either not be recognized or will be difficult to recognize. This fact is surprising when one considers that the relationship of parts of the figure to one another is not affected by such a change. It is clear that these geometrical relationships provide the essential information about form, and for this reason transpositions of retinal position or size do *not* alter perceived shape. Why, then, do transpositions of orientation have this effect?

There are, however, two separate consequences of varying a figure's orientation in the frontal plane: the orientation of the retinal image as well as the orientation of the figure with respect to the environment are changed. Although both kinds of change ordinarily occur when a figure is disoriented, they can be separated experimentally in various ways. To consider only the effect of changing the orientation of the retinal image, a simple method

125

is to view a figure which remains upright in the environment with the head in a tilted (or inverted) position. To consider only the effect of changing the orientation of the figure in the environment, one can view a tilted figure with the head tilted by an equal amount.

When experiments are done to determine the separate effect of these two factors, the results indicate that for a novel figure there is little change in appearance when only the orientation of its retinal image is changed. On the other hand, when the orientation of the figure in the environment is changed, it is generally perceived as different and may not be recognized. This phenomenal change depends upon the fact that the observer organizes the figure in such a way that the region which is uppermost in the environment is taken to be its top (and so forth with respect to its bottom, left, and right sides). If instead, he realizes that the figure is now tilted into a new orientation, the chances are he will recognize it. Findings of this kind suggest that what matters is not so much the orientation of the figure in the environment but the fact that normally one "assigns" the directions top, bottom, left, and right to a figure on the basis of information provided by cues, such as the visual frame of reference or gravity, concerning what is "top" and "bottom" in the environment. The evidence indicates that it is a change in the assignment of these directions to a figure that profoundly affects its shape. Various other factors can influence how these directions are assigned, such as instructions or set; one's own egocentric sense of "up" and "down," which can be isolated by viewing a figure in a horizontal plane; intrinsic properties of the figure; or familiarity with a figure.

Phenomenal shape is affected by such assignment of directions because the implicit cognitive description of a figure is a function of the figure's directions: whether a figure's long axis is "vertical" or "horizontal"; whether the figure rests on a base or stands on a point; whether it is symmetrical or not, and so forth.

The effect on perceived form of varying degrees of angular change in the assignment of directions is different for each figure, but, in general, it tends to be maximal for changes of 45 and 90°. It is minimal for left–right reversals. In the latter case, the description of the figure as a function of orientation is virtually unchanged.

The effect of altering the directions assigned to a figure is not restricted to vision. Forms that are experienced only tactually are often not recognized when they are rotated without the observer's knowledge.

In general, a disoriented figure will not be recognized unless the observer achieves the correct assignment of directions (by one means or another), or unless the new orientation does not alter phenomenal shape very much, as in a left–right reversal.

It is a fact, however, that certain material, such as printed or written words and faces, is difficult to recognize when there is no change in the assignment of directions but when the orientation of the retinal image is altered. For example, we cannot recognize cursively written words when the head is inverted, despite the fact that we remain aware of the location of the top and bottom of the word. Thus, there is also a retinal orientation factor that affects the perception of form, but it seems to show up only with certain kinds of material and for appreciable degrees of retinal disorientation.

It was suggested that this factor is a function of the difficulty in perceiving certain kinds of figures because the directions assigned to them are not in alignment with the observer's retinally determined egocentric coordinates. For example, in viewing a figure with one's head inverted, the egocentric "uppermost" direction of the figure is the region which is taken to be its bottom on the basis of various sources of information about up and down in the environment. Ordinarily this lack of alignment has little if any effect on perceived form, because a process of correction occurs analogous to the process that takes place in other cases of perceptual constancy. This process entails superseding the percept based on the retinal–egocentric coordinates by one based on directions assigned in accordance with available information about the location of the true top, bottom, and sides of the figure. It necessitates visualization of what the figure would look like were it aligned with the egocentric coordinates.

For certain kinds of stimulus material such as word figures or faces, the process of correction is unsuccessful because there are too many subparts and relationships among such parts, all of which must be corrected at once if perception is to be adequate. Subparts and relationships that are not corrected are perceived on the basis of egocentrically determined assigned directions. An experiment with quadrilateral figures demonstrated that when several retinally disoriented figures were viewed in a brief test exposure, recognition fell off appreciably in comparison with upright test figures. There was insufficient time to correct the several retinally inverted test figures.

The greater the degree of retinal disorientation, or, otherwise expressed, the greater the degree of nonalignment of assigned figural directions and egocentric coordinates, the greater the difficulty of perception. This may be a function of the increasing difficulty of visualization or mental rotation with increasing difference between egocentric and figural coordinates.

There appear to be two components to the retinal factor. One is the result of the difficulty of correction as explained above. Consequently, an impairment of recognition will occur if the figure is not egocentrically upright even when it is in the *same* retinal orientation in both training and test. It is this component which reflects progressive disturbance as a function of degree of retinal disorientation. The other component is a further disturbance based on a *change* of retinal orientation from training to test. This may be the result of depriving the observer of the possibility of recognizing the figure on the basis of the uncorrected egocentrically determined percept, so that he can only recognize on the basis of the corrected percept. In other words, when the observer is tilted by the same amount in both training and test, he has a possible dual basis for recognition, one based on the uncorrected retinally determined percept and its trace, the other based on the corrected percept and its trace. But when the observer is tilted in training and upright in the test or vice versa, he can only recognize the figure on the basis of the corrected percept and its trace because the uncorrected percept and its trace are different from one another.

Thus both factors may be reduced to the effect of subjectively assigned directions on phenomenal shape. The assignment of direction factor results from a direct change in this assignment. The retinal factor results from a primitive tendency to assign directions on the basis of retinal (and therefore) egocentric coordinates. As a result, a process of correction is necessary, and for certain material in certain orientations this correction is difficult: it becomes difficult to perceive in terms of the directions that are called for.

Various theories about the effect of orientation on form perception were considered in the light of the findings reported here. For the most part, they do not do justice to the facts because they fail to distinguish between effects based on change in assignment of direction and those based on difficulty of correction necessitated by retinal change.

The implications of the data and conclusions concerning orientation for a general theory of form perception and recognition were examined. It was suggested that form perception is not to be understood as more or less synonymous with contour formation (as is now widely believed to be the case), but as the synthesis of a set of perceived locations. Evidence to support this view was presented. The synthesis consists of an act of implicitly "describing" (in nonverbal terms) the locations of the parts of the figure relative to one another. The "description" also gives special weight to salient features of the configuration and includes reference to the characteristics of the figure in relation to its top, bottom, and sides. A number of facts about form perception that concern complexity, attention, transposition, and the like can be understood on the basis of cognitive description.

As for recognition, which is based on similarity of percept to memory trace, the findings on orientation suggest that in addition to internal geometrical relationships and other features of a figure, the "description" of a figure, which determines what memory traces will be judged similar to it, also includes features bearing on orientation. If directions are now assigned differently to a figure than before (even when the orientation of the image is unchanged), then the figure will look different and will therefore not be recognized. Conversely, it generally will be recognized despite retinal change if there is no change in the directions assigned to it.

★

★  ★

# Appendix

### Details of the Experiment on
### Degree of Orientation Change and Perceived Shape[1]

*Procedure*

Each observer inspected some figures during training when
he was upright, and other figures when his head was tilted 45°
clockwise, when it was tilted 90° clockwise, and when he was inverted 180°. When he was upright in training, he was also shown
some figures that were left–right reversed from their upright
orientation, and when he was inverted in training, he was shown
some figures that were inverted rather than rotated 180°. The
purpose of these two conditions was to obtain data on two types
of orientation change that are not simply the result of rotation

[1]Conducted by Phyllis Olshansky; see pages 26–34.

in a frontal plane, namely, a left–right reversal and an up–down inversion. Both of these necessarily do entail a change in the figure's retinal orientation, but to minimize it for the up–down condition, the observer was inverted too. Finally, as a control, each observer saw some figures in training when tilted 90° clockwise and saw just these figures in the test when he was also tilted 90° clockwise. The figures of course, remained in the same orientation both times. In this case, therefore, there was no *change* of orientation from training to test of any kind. The purpose was to ascertain if the abnormal postures used in training had an adverse effect on subsequent recognition by virtue of discomfort, or the like. The order of degree of tilt in training and of specific figures in both training and test was systematically counterbalanced. The training figures were exposed for 2 sec each, and the test figures for 5 sec.

Since we wished to determine the effect of varying degrees of tilt on the recognizability of *each figure separately,* and since a given figure could be tested for only one degree of change of tilt for each observer, it was necessary to use a great many observers. By doing so, we ended up with 21 observers being tested for each degree of orientation change for each figure.

The figures were selected on the basis of several criteria (see Fig. 69), such as the desire to include various kinds of figures (simple and complex, open and closed, rectilinear and curvilinear), and the desire to test several hypotheses (for example, the role of symmetry, complexity, stability or balance, and elongation of the axis).

*Training*

Experimental figures were presented by slide projector. The subject was seated at the side of the table, on which the projector was located. The following instructions were read to him:

The first part of this experiment will deal with aesthetic judgments. I am going to show you some figures which

I want you to rate on a scale running from one to five. Rate each figure *one* if you find it extremely pleasing and *five* if you find it extremely unpleasing. Ratings of *two, three* or *four* will fall in between, depending upon your feeling about each figure.

Although I will ask you to tilt your head, every figure that I show you will be upright. For each figure that you see, the top will be where it normally is in the room. Remember (pointing) the top of this screen will always be the top of the figure, no matter how your head is tilted.

When I ask you to tilt your head 45°, please place your right cheek flush against this triangle. When I ask you to tilt your head 90°, lean your head flat on the table. For some figures you will need to invert your head. To do this, you will have to look at the screen by bending over and looking through your legs.

I will show you one figure at a time, each for a short period. Keep looking at each for the full exposure period, that is, don't look away until the figure goes off the screen, and then give me your rating quickly in the time given between figures. Any questions?

Okay, here's the first figure. Rate it from *one* to *five* and remember that even though your head may be tilted, the figures themselves will always be upright. (Pointing to the top of the screen.) This will always be the top of the figure.

The purpose of the aesthetic ratings was to guard against the subject's attempt to commit any figure to memory. During the training series, 14 novel figures plus 14 figures of familiar objects were each shown for an exposure period of 2 sec. Each subject was shown two different experimental slides while he and the slide were at 0, 45, 90, and 180°, a control pair for which subject and slide were both at 90°, a left–right reversal experimental pair for which the subject was at 0° and an inverted experimental pair for which the subject was at 180°. The left–

right reversal orientation (or L–R) involved a mirror-image reversal of the 0° slide around a vertical axis, for example, ⋏ at
0° became ⋏ at L–R. The inverted orientation involved a
mirror-image reversal of the 0° slide around a horizontal axis,
for example, ⋏ at 0° became ⋎ when inverted, while it became ⋎ at 180°.

To illustrate the training situation, a particular subject saw
slides (1a) and (1b) of Fig. 69 in an inverted position while he
was at 180°; slides (2a) and (2b) with both slides and self at 180°;
slides (3a) and (3b) with slides and self at 0°; slides (4a) and (4b)
at the control orientation with self and slides at 90°; slides (5a)
and (5b) with both slides and self at 45°; slides (6a) and (6b) with
both slides and self at 90°; and slides (7a) and (7b) with slides
left–right reversed and the self upright. (The name given to
each of these figures in Fig. 69 refers either to the sources of that
figure or the rationale for including it.) In addition to these,
14 slides of familiar objects were shown mixed in with the
others, and with these familiar slides, subject and slide were
always at 0°. The purpose of including such slides was to rein-
force the instructions to the effect that the top of the screen
was the top of the picture. Four separately determined and randomly arranged orders of presentation of these 28 slides were
used for each of the seven conditions of 21 subjects each, so that
only five or six subjects received the same slides in the same
order. The (a) and (b) slides of each pair in Fig. 69, however, were
always presented together in sequence. Seven conditions were
used, so that each of the 14 experimental figures were seen by 21
subjects at each of the seven different orientations.

*Test*

Two minutes after the training series, a test series was presented for the 14 novel figures. The following instructions were
first read:

Now, we will test for your ability to recognize the figures shown before during the aesthetics test. The figures you are about to see may or may not have been shown before. Say "yes" only if the figure now to be shown appears to be a figure shown before. Otherwise you are to respond "no." Remember, again, that this (pointing to top of screen) will always be the top of the figure.

During this test series, the 14 novel figures were again shown, but this time at a 0° orientation with the subject also at 0° (except for the control pair of slides, for which slides and self were both at 90° as in training). Interspersed with the 14 novel figures were 10 slides of familiar objects, different from those used in training. Again, the purpose of these slides was further reinforcement of the deceptive directions, which asked subjects to consider the top of the screen the top also of each figure. To repeat, figures in the test were presented in the same position retinally as in training, with the exception of slides given left–right reversed and inverted. Each test figure was shown for .5 sec. All responses of "yes" and "no," plus any relevant comments, were recorded. In the test as in the training series, for each of the seven conditions there were four prearranged random presentation orders, so that only five or six subjects of the 21 saw the same slides in the same order.

Following the test, an inquiry was conducted in which the subject was questioned to determine whether any of his "no" responses meant that he had recognized the figure, but thought "no" was appropriate because its orientation was now different.

*Results*

Table 6 presents the number and proportion of recognitions per figure out of a possible 21 per cell at each of the different orientations.

(1a)
Ethiopic letter 1

(1b)
Fragmented 1

(2a)
Symmetrical complex

(2b)
Balance 1

(3a)
Asymmetrical complex

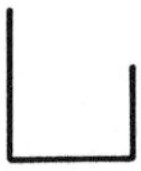

(3b)
Right angle

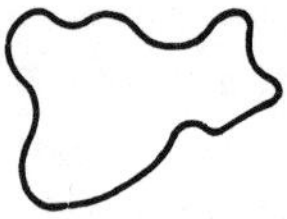

(4a)
Arnoult

(4b)
Vertical

(5a)
Ethiopic letter 2

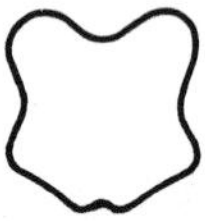

(5b)
Symmetrical simple

(6a)
Horizontal

(6b)
Asymmetrical simple

(7a)
Balance 2

(7b)
Fragmented 2

**FIG. 69**

**TABLE 6**

Number and Proportion of Subjects Recognizing Slide

| No. slide | Orientation | | | | | | | Mean proportion |
|---|---|---|---|---|---|---|---|---|
| | 0° | 45° | 90° | 180° | Inverted | Left–right reversal | Control | |
| 1a | 18(.86) | 11(.52) | 8(.38) | 13(.62) | 16(.76) | 16(.76) | 17(.81) | .67 |
| 1b | 15(.71) | 11(.52) | 15(.71) | 10(.48) | 11(.52) | 14(.67) | 15(.71) | .62 |
| 2a | 19(.90) | 13(.62) | 15(.71) | 20(.95) | 16(.76) | 19(.90) | 19(.90) | .82 |
| 2b | 21(1.00) | 16(.76) | 11(.52) | 19(.90) | 18(.86) | 17(.81) | 19(.90) | .82 |
| 3a | 19(.90) | 16(.76) | 19(.90) | 19(.90) | 17(.81) | 18(.86) | 19(.90) | .86 |
| 3b | 18(.86) | 11(.52) | 11(.52) | 13(.62) | 9(.43) | 16(.76) | 15(.71) | .63 |
| 4a | 17(.81) | 14(.67) | 7(.33) | 13(.62) | 12(.57) | 16(.76) | 17(.81) | .65 |
| 4b | 19(.90) | 9(.43) | 10(.48) | 17(.81) | 16(.76) | 15(.71) | 18(.86) | .71 |
| 5a | 18(.86) | 15(.71) | 19(.90) | 16(.76) | 13(.62) | 18(.86) | 16(.76) | .78 |
| 5b | 18(.86) | 11(.52) | 13(.62) | 18(.86) | 13(.62) | 20(.95) | 18(.86) | .76 |
| 6a | 17(.81) | 9(.43) | 6(.29) | 9(.43) | 18(.86) | 14(.67) | 16(.76) | .61 |
| 6b | 19(.90) | 19(.90) | 19(.90) | 17(.81) | 19(.90) | 17(.81) | 18(.86) | .87 |
| 7a | 19(.90) | 6(.29) | 13(.62) | 17(.81) | 13(.62) | 16(.76) | 18(.86) | .69 |
| 7b | 15(.70) | 10(.48) | 11(.52) | 15(.71) | 9(.43) | 16(.76) | 16(.76) | .62 |
| Mean number | 18.0 | 12.2 | 12.6 | 15.4 | 14.3 | 16.6 | 17.2 | |
| Mean proportion | .86 | .58 | .60 | .74 | .68 | .79 | .82 | |
| SD (proportion) | .07 | .16 | .20 | .16 | .16 | .08 | .07 | |

*Comment*

There are certain difficulties inherent in the method employed in this experiment that should be noted. The intention was that the observer would always assign the direction "top" to the region of the figure that was uppermost on the screen. Hence, it was expected that there would be a change in the directions assigned to a figure from training to test because the figure on the screen was oriented differently in training and test (in all but the 0° change condition and the control condition). Presumably, the combined cues of gravity, visual frame of reference, instructions, and the effect of upright familiar figures interspersed in the series would unambiguously lead to this assignment of "top."

Nevertheless, there are reasons why this may not have always taken place. During training, an observer may occasionally have shifted the perceived top of a figure to a region congruent with his own body position, particularly when he was inverted. Under certain conditions, one's egocentric coordinates do form the basis of assignment of directions to a figure. Whether camouflaging the purpose of the training exposure as a test of aesthetic judgment limited such a tendency is not certain, although it did tend to minimize the use of mnemonic aids or verbal description. Another possibility is that during the test, observers may occasionally have searched for the top of the figure and not simply accepted the spatial cues and instructions to the effect that the top was at the uppermost region of the figure. This could be expected to happen with increasing frequency as the test progressed, because the observer could realize that many figures that had been seen before were in fact being shown in a new orientation. There is evidence that such a trend did develop.

The net result of either or both of these occurrences would be successful recognition of figures for the obvious reason that, psychologically speaking, the orientation would then be unchanged from training to test. Thus, the results obtained are conservative. Had there been no such cases, recognition would have been poorer for all conditions of orientation change. Based on interview data obtained after the experiment, however, there is reason to think that such instances were the exception. There is one tendency, however, that would work in the opposite direction, namely, to decrease recognition. An observer in the test might recognize a figure but also see that its orientation was different from that of the training period. He might then feel he should say "no," that it was not the figure shown in the training period. Again, however, whereas the interview confirmed that such cases occurred, they were clearly the exception.

## Details of the Quadrilateral-Figure Experiment[2]

*Procedure*

The following instructions were read to the subject.

> This is an experiment in visual perception. I'm going to show you a simple geometric figure and let you memorize it. Then I'm going to show you a series of four cards, each of which has four figures on it. The four figures may or may not include the figure that you memorized. The figure you memorized will be called the training figure, and the cards that follow it will be called the test cards. If you think that a particular test card does not have the training figure on it, simply say "none" or "no." If you think that a training figure is on a particular test card, I want you to specify which of the four figures you think that it is. You can easily do this because a card with four colored dots will appear immediately after the test card goes off. One colored dot will be in the position of each figure, so if you think, for instance, that the top right-hand figure is the one which you memorized and there is a blue dot in that position, simply say "blue."

[2]Conducted by Charles Bebber and Douglas Blewett; see pages 53–56.

Now if you look into the machine, you will see a black dot. The training figure will always appear approximately where that dot is, and the test figure will be arrayed around the dot. It is important to fixate on that dot before the cards appear, since you will have only three seconds to memorize the training figure and only one second to see the test figure.

The test figures that you see will all be somewhat similar to the figure that you memorized, but it does not count as the same unless it is *exactly* the same in all respects. In other words, if a test figure is not the same size or shape, or if it is tilted differently from the training figure, it does not count as the same figure. Now I'll give you some practice cards so that you'll have a better idea of what you're to do. I'll give you a three second exposure of the training figure before *each* of the four test cards. (Demonstration.)

Now, there is one other thing I'd like you to do. In this experiment, you'll see four sets of training and test cards. For two of the sets, I'd like you to have your head upside down, rather than the way you just saw the cards. You will always learn the training figures right-side up, but half of the time you will see the test figures with your head upside down. Remember, it is only your head which will be upside down; the figures will always be right side up, so you will have to take that into consideration when you are trying to see if the training figure is there or not. Let's try some practice cards with your head upside down. After each test card, you can be seated to get another 3-sec exposure of the training figure. (Demonstration.)

Now we're ready for the experiment. I'll give you one hint about the experiment. You're going to see 16 test cards altogether, and eight of the cards will have the training figure, while eight will not. In other words, if you were 100% correct, you would be giving me "none" for an answer on eight of the cards and a color on the other eight cards. If you are pretty sure that you know an answer, take a guess, but if you absolutely don't know at all, you can say so. Do you have any questions?

Each training figure was shown twice in succession each time for 3 sec. Two of the four test cards for each training figure were positive (that is, contained the training figure) and two were negative. Following the sequence of two training exposures (which were always with head upright) and four test cards, another training figure was exposed twice, followed by the four test cards pertaining to it, and so forth. Altogether, each observer saw four training figures and, therefore, 16 test cards. For two of the training figures, the observer's head was inverted during presentation of the four test cards. Factors such as position of the correct figure on the card, order of figures, and figure assigned to upright and inverted testing were systematically varied.

The method by which the test cards were constructed was as follows, using Figs. 42 and 43 (page 54) as an example. The figure at the left in Fig. 43 was derived by exchanging the lengths of the two sides of the training figure resulting in a change of slope of the top line; the figure at the upper left is the training figure; the one at the lower right was derived by inverting the training figure and distorting it somewhat; and the one at the upper right was derived by exchanging the lengths of the top and bottom lines. For negative cards, the fourth figure was the mirror image of the training figure. This plan was followed in constructing all test cards.

The subjects were 16 college students.

## Results

The mean score was 4.5 for the upright test position and 2.25 for the inverted position. Table 7 gives the results separately

**TABLE 7**
MEAN NUMBER OF TEST CARDS RECOGNIZED

|          | Positive cards | Negative cards |
|----------|:--------------:|:--------------:|
| Upright  | 2.1            | 2.4            |
| Inverted | 1.0            | 1.2            |

for positive and negative cards. The maximum score per cell was 4. The superiority of upright over inverted test position held for each training figure.

*Comment*

If subjects made "color" and "no" responses equally frequently to all test cards, then chance performance would be 50% for negative cards and 12.5% for positive cards. This is so because a subject would be correct half the time on negative cards merely by guessing "no" half the time. On positive cards, if he guessed "yes" half the time, he would be potentially correct by chance half the time, but he would then have to guess the correct color and his chance of doing so would be one in four. Therefore, the probability of being correct by guessing the correct color would be .50 × .25, or .125. However, the analysis is complicated by the fact that for all the cards combined, subjects made color responses 64% of the time and "no" responses 36% of the time. Taking this fact into account, chance becomes 36% for negative cards and 16% for positive cards. Therefore, on a chance basis the scores for positive cards in Table 7 would be 16% of 4, or .64, and for negative cards, 36% of 4, or 1.44. Thus, it appears that performance on positive or negative cards seen from an upright position is well above chance; on cards seen from an inverted position performance is only somewhat above chance for positive cards and is slightly below chance for negative cards.

CONTROL EXPERIMENT: ONE TEST FIGURE AT A TIME[3]

*Procedure*

The subject saw two training figures in succession, each for 1 sec. He then worked on a puzzle for 2 min. This was followed by eight test figures, all of which were seen with head upright or with head inverted. Among the eight test figures were the two training figures just seen, three incorrect figures similar to one of the training figures, and three similar to the other training figure. The order of these eight test cards was randomized. Then there followed the two other training figures, another 2-min session with a puzzle, and then the eight test cards for the training figures. If the previous test cards had been seen with head upright, these eight were seen with head inverted or vice versa. Test cards were shown for 1 sec. All these changes of exposure time and sequence of events were introduced with one purpose, namely, to keep the task from being so easy that there would be few errors when the subject was upright. Such a result would have made it difficult to interpret scores obtained under the inverted condition.

The subjects were 14 college students.

*Results*

The mean number correct in the upright position was 5.8; in the inverted position it was 5.6. If only positive cards are considered, where the maximum score correct per condition is 2, the means were 1.35 and 1.28 for upright and inverted conditions respectively. Thus, it is clear there is no difference between the upright and inverted conditions of testing.

[3]See pages 56–57.

## VARIATION: SUBJECTS INVERTED IN TRAINING AND TEST[4]

The procedure followed that of the main experiment and is adequately described on pages 64–65. The results given on page 64 are based on 12 subjects. However, the experiment subsequently was repeated with 16 subjects.[4] In this revision, a few changes were inadvertently introduced so that the results cannot be directly compared to those of the other quadrilateral-figure experiments. The exposure time for the test cards was 2 sec instead of 1. Nevertheless, the results confirm the fact that recognition is significantly superior for figures seen from an upright position in training and test (mean number correct, 5.6) than for figures seen from an inverted position in training and test (mean number correct, 3.4).

## VARIATION: SUBJECTS TILTED 90° IN TEST[5]

The procedure followed that of the main experiment with the single exception that half the figures were now seen from an upright position in training and with the head tilted 90° in the test. The other half of the figures were seen from an upright position in training and test.

The subjects were 26 college students.

### An Experiment with Novel Figures Employing a Fine-Discrimination Test

There is one combination of factors that we have found to affect recognition of retinally disoriented figures, which does not depend on either extreme retinal disorientation *or* complexity. An experiment was designed based on the assumption

[4]Performed by Steven Koncsol.
[5]See pages 69–70.

that when retinal change is involved, what one can reasonably expect is not so much a gross change in the perceived shape of a figure, but rather some difficulty in discriminating it from other like figures. Since inverted words and faces are still recognized as words and faces, a description of the difficulty in these cases is the inability to *read* words (discriminate them from other words) and the inability to make out which face one is looking at or what its expression is. With this in mind, in one of our studies of the retinal factor, the observer was required to make a fine discrimination in the recognition test. For each of the 12 figures shown in training (for 10 sec) a test card was made up consisting of one correct and other quite similar figures. Figure 70 is an illustration of one such figure and its test card. The test card was exposed for 15 sec, long enough to permit the observer to survey the alternatives and make a selection. Several other of the figures employed in this experiment are shown in Figs. 40 and 41 (page 52). All combinations of the following orientations of the observer in training and in test were employed: 0, 45, 90, and 180°. The figures themselves were always upright, and the observer knew this.

We found that with this method of testing, there was a decline in recognition for all degrees of head tilt, as compared to a control condition where the observer remained upright. The magnitude of the decline was between 10 and 30%. However, when the experiment was repeated but only one or two figures

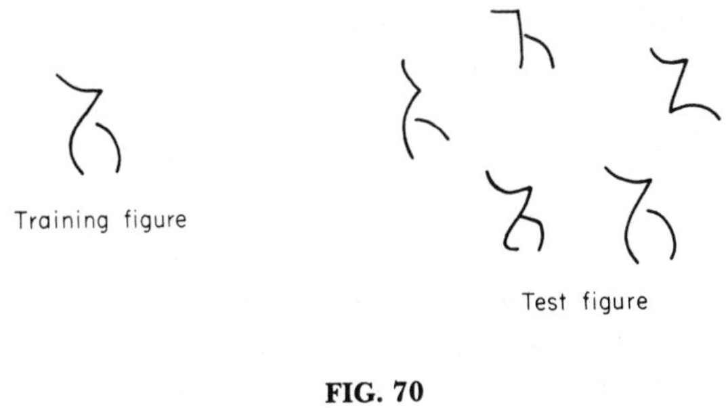

Training figure

Test figure

**FIG. 70**

were shown in training and then tested, there was no effect on recognition of retinal orientation.

The analysis given in Figs. 49, 50, and 51 (pages 66 and 67, respectively) may provide an explanation of these findings. It should first be noted that even relatively simple figures evidenced the decline in recognition when the observer was tilted, though correction should not have been difficult to achieve. The problem is to understand why conditions of interference generated by the use of many figures might have a *differential effect* on figures seen by an upright observer and a tilted observer. The answer may be that when the observer is tilted, two traces are formed of each figure, one based on correction and one on the uncorrected, egocentrically determined percept. However, each of the two traces formed may be thought to be somewhat weaker or less stable than the one trace of the "good" percept occurring when the observer is upright. A corrected percept, even if successful, entails a process of visualization and thus may not leave behind as adequate a trace as does a percept that does not require correction. The other trace, of the egocentrically determined percept, would not be very strong because it results from a percept that is superseded and not in the forefront of experience. The fact that these two traces are relatively weak may not be of any consequence unless the conditions are such that memory is particularly vulnerable. The interference generated by the use of many figures could constitute just such a condition.

In this same experiment, several conditions were included where the observer was in the *same* rotated position in training and in test. Recognition declined in these conditions in comparison with the condition where the observer was upright throughout. This finding would seem to support the explanation proposed above—that the trace of the corrected percept is not as good as that of the percept which doesn't require correction. For in these conditions, recognition can also occur on the basis of the identity between uncorrected, egocentrically determined trace and percept (as outlined in Fig. 49, page 66). But, in spite of this possible advantage, recognition declined.[6]

## Details of an Experiment
## on the Recognition of Familiar Material
## as a Function of Degree of Disorientation[7]

Words were exposed for 2 sec, faces for 2 sec, and fragmented figures for 20 sec. Since already familiar material was used, no training period was necessary. The observer viewed four examples of words, four examples of faces, and three examples of fragmented figures when upright, when tilted 45° clockwise, when tilted 90° clockwise, and when inverted. The faces were those of John Kennedy, Franklin Roosevelt, Fred Astaire, and Steve Allen. The words were "cordial," "untimely," "quiescent," and "scarcely"; the fragmented figures were a car, a ship, and a horse and carriage. There were 64 different observers in each of the test positions. Since each observer saw four figures per category, the maximum score for each category was 256. (The fragmented figure scores were corrected to conform to this base line of 4.) The results are given in Fig. 52 (page 69).

## The Perception of Fragmented Figures

We have performed experiments in which fragmented figures of the kind shown in Fig. 71 were viewed by observers whose heads were tilted 90° (Rock & Heimer, 1957). Recognition was

---

[6]The experiments described here were conducted by Edna Ortof (1966) and George Steinfeld. The interested reader is referred to Steinfeld's doctoral dissertation (1968). On pp. 33–41 of the dissertation, the research referred to above entailing conditions of interference is described. See also Steinfeld (1970).

[7]Conducted by George Steinfeld; see page 69.

slightly, but significantly, poorer than when the observers were upright. Since this is the case, some attempt to explain this fact is warranted.

Unfortunately, we know very little about the mechanism underlying the perception of fragmented figures. Typically, a perceptual reorganization occurs, because at first the figure looks like a meaningless jumble of fragments. Then suddenly it is recognized as representing a familiar thing and it is perceived differently. The transformation is not unlike a sudden insight in problem solving. The reader may experience this effect in viewing Fig. 71. What accounts for the perceptual change that leads to recognition is not known, but one possibility is that a part of the pattern is recognized first, for example a hand, and that provides the clue as to what the whole pattern is. It is also known that prior experience with the pattern that culminates in successful recognition will carry over and permit almost instantaneous rerecognition at a later time (Leeper, 1935). But again, we do not know the mechanism underlying this effect.

In the light of such ignorance about the basis of perception of these figures when they are upright, it is not likely that we can unravel what takes place—or fails to take place—when they are disoriented. Of course, if there is a change in the as-

**FIG. 71**

signment of directions to such a figure, as occurred in some experiments described in Chapter IV (pages 47–48), then there is nothing at all mysterious about the failure of recognition. With the observer in error about where the top of the array is, there is little reason to expect the necessary perceptual reorganization to take place.

More problematical are cases involving the retinal factor, where the observer is aware of the true location of the top, and so forth, as, for example, when the figures remain upright and are viewed from a tilted body position. A few comments and speculations may be ventured. First, the fragmented figures we have used generally represent rather complex objects or combinations of objects. Therefore, even if a *completed* silhouette of the object were presented, rather than a fragmented one, there would undoubtedly still be a disturbance with retinal disorientation. To that extent the cause of the difficulty would perhaps be similar to that which gives rise to the difficulty in recognizing face figures.

But no doubt the fragmentation of the figures adds considerably to the difficulty. As far as original recognition is concerned, if the speculation above about the role of parts is correct, then, with retinal disorientation, each part must be corrected before *it* itself can be recognized. Since there are many such parts, any one of which might be the essential clue, it is entirely possible that this necessary first step would fail to occur. This explanation could therefore explain our results.

However, there is reason to believe that the proper perception of such figures is adversely affected by disorientation, even in rerecognition. In fact, if one inverts a figure that, when upright, is properly recognized, it will be difficult to make it out even though one is perfectly aware of what it is. If the reader has by now recognized Fig. 71 as a couple dancing, he can experience the difficulty referred to here by inverting it. This points up a fact about the perception of fragmented figures not yet sufficiently emphasized, namely, that the perceptual transition from

initial meaningless jumble to familiar object is not merely one of
coming to realize what the jumble represents. There is a genuine
perceptual change concomitant with—or possibly immediately
*prior to*—the recognition. Each part of the array falls into place,
so to speak, and is perceived as some part of the whole. There is
also a completing or filling in between the fragments. This is adversely affected when an already recognized figure is inverted, just
as with word figures which change even when rotated right before
the eyes.

Therefore, the cause of the disturbance here is no longer that
a part fails to suggest what the whole might be. Rather, there
appears to be a difficulty with the correction process entailing
the entire figure much as is the case for words and faces. Again,
some of this difficulty would be present even for nonfragmented
pictures of this kind. The specific nature of the additional difficulty with fragmented figures, however, may result from the
necessity of a double process of visualization. First, the observer
must visualize how the components and their relationships
would look if they were egocentrically upright. Then, however,
he must visualize how the fragments are integrated with one
another to form the whole, since it is a fragmented figure. When
the figure is upright, the second process must occur, but when
it is disoriented, both processes must occur.

## Experiments on Reading
## Orientationally Transformed Words and Letters[8]

In a series of carefully executed experiments, Kolers and
Perkins have examined the effect on speed of reading or letter-
naming of various kinds of orientational transformations (Kolers,
1968; Kolers & Perkins, 1969a, b). The text was presented normally, rotated 180°, inverted, and left–right reversed. In addition,

[8]Conducted by Paul Kolers and David Perkins.

in each of these conditions, individual letters also were reversed. The various transformations were read from left to right as well as right to left. For text, the order of increasing difficulty was normal, rotated, inverted, and reversed (although there was little difference between the last two). With letter reversals in addition to the word transformations, the order of difficulty was somewhat different. For letter naming, the order of increasing difficulty was normal, rotated, reversed, and inverted. A particularly interesting finding in letter naming was that the rightward or normal direction of scanning printed English material was not always faster than the leftward direction. Direction of scanning interacted with type of transformation. Namely, if letters faced rightward, then rightward scanning was indeed more rapid; if letters faced leftward, however, then leftward scanning was more rapid. The investigators view their findings as supporting a theory that considers perception to be the result of a constructive process of problem solving. In the case of disoriented material, the operation of rectificational mechanisms is required.

In these experiments, no distinction was made between assignment of direction and retinal change. Words and letters were transformed both with respect to environmental and to retinal directions. However, it is safe to assume that with the immediate recognition of the nature of the material, the observer is aware of the altered location of the top, bottom, left, and right of the letters and words, so that by and large we are dealing here with the problem of attempted correction or, in short, the retinal factor.

In the experiments described in the present monograph, retinal change is generally the results of a changed orientation of the observer to the figure by rotation of the observer about an axis orthogonal to the plane of the figure. This kind of transformation was emphasized for two reasons: (1) because it is one that occurs often in daily life, and (2) because a tilted observer who views upright figures is provided with direct *perceptual* information concerning their true top and bottom via gravity and visual frame of reference. Some of the transformations Kolers and Perkins studied are rare in daily life, requiring reflections from glass or mirrors or seeing a two-dimensional object from the opposite side (reversals), or seeing such an object flipped upside down or from the opposite side after it is rotated (inversions). The more complicated separate transformations of letters within words and, at the same time, words as a whole could never occur naturally.

Furthermore, these transformations do not provide direct perceptual cues, as is the case with upright figures viewed by a tilted observer. Without great familiarity with the material or instructions, there would be no reason to correct a left–right reversed figure or an inverted one. Therefore, if such trans-formations were to be imposed upon *novel* material, we could not separate the assignment of direction factor from the retinal factor, unless we instructed the observer about the correct orientation.

Still, these transformations are possible and, therefore, Kolers' and Perkins' data provide us with new factual information about the difficulty of correction in these cases. If it is right to think that correction requires visualizing how a figure would appear if its top, bottom, and sides conformed to the egocentric coordinates, then reversal requires visualizing the figure to be turned around its vertical axis by 180°, or visualizing ourselves to turn around and face the figure from the opposite side. It is interesting to relate this analysis to what was said earlier (page 33) about left–right re-versal as a type of *phenomenal* change. There it was argued that such a transformation ought not to affect phenomenal shape very much because it is essentially an exchange of the sides of the figure. The findings in the study conducted by Olshansky (and those of other investigators) support this expectation. However, if a figure that is asymmetrical about its vertical axis has become *very familiar* (such as certain letters of the alphabet), reversing it would no doubt cause it to look quite strange. We have learned that certain features are on its left and others on its right side. Given this fact, it is no longer a contradiction to find that correction is necessary, and the process of correction for reversed material may well be difficult relative to what is required for other kinds of transformations.

It is not easy to unravel the many factors at work in Kolers' and Perkins' experiments. First, there is the possible role of past experience. Of the various transformations, only rotation is one that is frequently encountered, and this might possibly explain why this was the easiest one to cope with. Second, in reading words, there is the difficulty of letter identification and the difficulty of identifying letter order. One would imagine that both together would prove more difficult than a transformation of either one alone. Thus, it is true that it is more difficult to read mirror-image words (Fig. 72a) than words where letters only are mirror image (Fig. 72b) or words the letter order of which is mirror imaged but the letters are normal (Fig. 72c). It is true that rotated words, entailing changed letter orientation and letter order (Fig. 72d), are easier to read than words where the letters only are rotated, and the letter order is normal (Fig. 72e). But when the entire word is rotated, the subject can try to visualize the entire word turned around and thus simultaneously correct letters and letter order. When only the letters are rotated, word recognition cannot be for the word as a whole, even following letter correction.

Finally, there is the question of direction of scanning. Clearly this is an additional complicating factor in the case of reading that is not more generally relevant to the problem of orientation in form perception. When scanning is required in viewing a figure—because it subtends too large an angle to be perceived

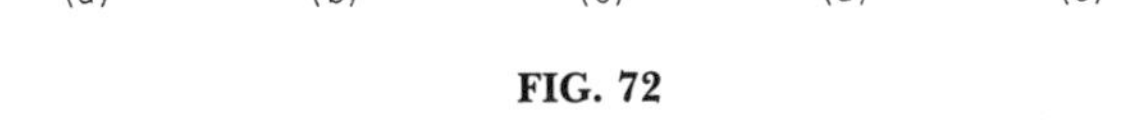

FIG. 72

with a single fixation—there is no prescribed direction for such scanning. For this reason, when we studied recognition of printed material, to avoid the problem of scanning we used only single words that could be apprehended without any eye movements at all. The same difficulty in decoding a disoriented word compared to an upright one would certainly be present in tachistoscopic exposures too brief to permit any eye movements. In normal reading, we are told that a cluster of several words apparently is read at a glance when the eye is stationary, before it jumps to its next position.

There is also the possibility of confusing the factor of direction of scanning with letter order. While moving the eyes leftward across a word, one can nevertheless be recognizing it on the basis of the correct location of letters in the left-to-right order. It is possible that when words or groups of letters are identified at a glance, the simultaneous awareness of letter order ("first," "second," "last") may make it difficult to pronounce them in a different order, as is required in Kolers' and Perkins' experiment involving leftward direction of scanning. These investigators point out that the direction in which letters face may affect the way in which they are ordered, and this, in turn, may conflict with the set concerning letter order derived from direction of scanning. Therefore, it is not clear what their results concerning direction of scanning mean, and it is of interest to note that in any case the contribution of this factor is small compared with the effect of transformation per se.

# References

Arnoult, M. D. Shape discrimination as a function of the angular orientation of the stimuli. *Journal of Experimental Psychology,* 1954, **47**, 323–328.

Attneave, F. Triangles as ambiguous figures. *American Journal of Psychology,* 1968, **81**, 447–453.

Attneave, F., & Olson, R. K. Discriminability of stimuli varying in physical and retinal orientation. *Journal of Experimental Psychology,* 1967, **74**, 149–157.

Attneave, F., & Reid, K. Voluntary control of frame of reference and shape equivalence under head rotation. *Journal of Experimental Psychology,* 1968, **78**, 153–159.

Aubert, H. Eine scheinbare bedeutende Drehung von Objekten bei Neigung des Kopfes nach rechts oder links. *Virchows Archiv,* 1861, **20**, 381–393.

Beck, J. Lightness and orientation. *American Journal of Psychology,* 1969, **82**, 359–366.

Begelman, D. A. The role of retinal orientation in the egocentric organization of a visual stimulus. *Journal of General Psychology,* 1968, **79**, 283–289.

Brooks, R. M., & Goldstein, A. G. Recognition by children of inverted photographs of faces. *Child Development,* 1963, **34**, 1033–1040.

Brown, J. F. The visual perception of velocity. *Psychologische Forschung,* 1931, **14**, 199–232.

155

Dearborn, G. V. N. Recognition under objective reversal. *Psychological Review,* 1899, **6**, 395–406.

Ebenholtz, S. Adaptation to a rotated visual field as a function of degree of optical tilt and exposure time. *Journal of Experimental Psychology,* 1966, **72,** 629–634.

Epstein, W., & De Shazo, D. Recency as a function of perceptual oscillation. *American Journal of Psychology,* 1961, **74,** 215–223.

Ghent, L. Recognition by children of realistic figures presented in various orientations. *Canadian Journal of Psychology,* 1960, **14,** 249–256.

Ghent, L. Form and its orientation: A child's-eye view. *American Journal of Psychology,* 1961, **74,** 177–190.

Ghent, L. Effect of orientation on recognition of geometric forms by retarded children. *Child Development,* 1964, **35,** 1127–1136.

Ghent, L., & Bernstein, L. Influence of the orientation of geometric forms on their recognition by children. *Perceptual and Motor Skills,* 1961, **12,** 95–101.

Gibson, J. J., & Gibson, E. J. Perceptual learning: Differentiation or enrichment? *Psychological Review,* 1955, **62,** 32–41.

Gibson, J. J., & Robinson, D. Orientation in visual perception: The recognition of familiar plane forms in differing orientations. *Psychology Monographs,* 1935, **46**(6, Whole No. 210).

Gibson, E. J., Gibson, J. J., Pick, A. D., & Osser, H. A developmental study of the discrimination of letter-like forms. *Journal of Comparative and Physiological Psychology,* 1962, **55,** 897–906.

Goldmeier, E. Über Ähnlichkeit bei gesehenen Figuren. *Psychologische Forschung,* 1937, **21,** 146–209; Translation (by Goldmeier): Similarity in visually perceived forms. *Psychological Issues,* 1972, **8,** No. 1, Monogr. 29, 1–135.

Hebb, E. O. *The organization of behavior.* New York: Wiley, 1949.

Hochberg, J. In the mind's eye. In R. N. Haber (Ed.), *Contemporary theory and research in visual perception.* New York: Holt, 1968. Pp. 309–331.

Howard, I. P., & Templeton, W. B. *Human spatial orientation.* New York: Wiley, 1966.

Hubel, D. H., & Wiesel, T. N. Receptive fields, binocular interaction, and functional architecture in the cat's visual cortex. *Journal of Physiology,* 1962, **160,** 106–123.

Julesz, B. *Foundations of cyclopean perception.* Chicago: University of Chicago Press, 1971.

Kanizsa, G. Margini quasi-percettivi in campi con stimolazioni omegenea. *Rivista di Psicologia,* 1955, **49,** 7–30.

Kanizsa, G., & Tampieri, G. Nouve osservazioni sull' orientamento retinico ed ambientale. In G. Kanizsa & G. Vicario (Eds.), *Ricerche sperimentali sulla percezione.* Trieste: Università degli Studi di Trieste, 1968.

Koffka, K. *Principles of gestalt psychology.* New York: Harcourt, 1935.

Köhler, W. *Dynamics in psychology.* New York: Liveright, 1940.

Köhler, W., & Wallach, H. Figural aftereffects; an investigation of visual processes. *Proceedings of the American Philosophical Society,* 1944, **88,** 269–357.

Kolers, P. A. The recognition of geometrically transformed text. *Perception & Psychophysics*, 1968, **3**, 57–64.

Kolers, P. A., & Perkins, D. N. Orientation of letters and errors in their recognition. *Perception & Psychophysics*, 1969, **5**, 265–269.  (a)

Kolers, P. A., & Perkins, D. N. Orientation of letters and their speed of recognition. *Perception & Psychophysics*, 1969, **5**, 275–280.  (b)

Kopfermann, H. Psychologische Untersuchungen über die Wirkung zweidimensionaler Darstellungen körperlicher Gebilde. *Psychologische Forschung*, 1930, **13**, 293–364.

Künnapas, T. M. Influence of head inclination on the vertical–horizontal illusion. *Journal of Psychology*, 1958, **46**, 179–185.

Leeper, R. A study of a neglected portion of the field of learning—the development of sensory organization. *Journal of Genetic Psychology*, 1935, **46**, 41–75.

Mach, E. *The analysis of sensations*. Chicago: Open Court, 1914. (Republished, New York: Dover, 1959.)

Mack, A., & Rock, I. A reexamination of the Stratton effect: Egocentric adaptation to a rotated visual image. *Perception & Psychophysics*, 1968, **4**, 57–62.

Mackintosh, N. J., Mackintosh, J., & Sutherland, N. S. The relative importance of horizontal and vertical extents in shape discrimination by octopus. *Animal Behavior*, 1963, **11**, 355–358.

Marshall, W. H., & Talbot, S. A. Recent evidence for neural mechanisms in vision leading to a general theory of sensory acuity. In J. Cattell (Ed.), *Biological symposia*. Vol. VII *Visual mechanisms* (H. Kluever, Ed.). Lancaster, Pennsylvania: Jacques Cattell Press, 1942. Pp. 117–164.

McGurk, H. The role of object orientation in infant perception. *Journal of Experimental Child Psychology*, 1970, **9**, 363–373.

McGurk, H. Infant discrimination of orientation. *Journal of Experimental Child Psychology*, 1972, **14**, 151–164.  (a)

McGurk, H. The salience of orientation in young children's perception of form. *Child Development*, 1972, **43**, 1047–1052.  (b)

Mikaelian, H., & Held, R. Two types of adaptation to an optically rotated visual field. *American Journal of Psychology*, 1964, **77**, 257–263.

Morinaga, S., Noguchi, K., & Ohishi, A. The horizontal–vertical illusion and the relation of spatial and retinal orientations. *Japanese Psychological Research*, 1962, **4**(1), 25–29.

Neisser, U. *Cognitive psychology*. New York: Appleton, 1966.

Olshansky, P. Phenomenal orientation in form perception. Unpublished paper, Yeshiva University, 1966.

Ortof, E. The effect of retinal disorientation on the recognition of different forms seen upright in the environment. Unpublished paper, Yeshiva University, 1966.

Pappalardo, S. A developmental study of form orientation and recognition. Doctoral thesis, Yeshiva University, 1966.

Rice, C. The orientation of plane figures as a factor in their perception by children. *Child Development*, 1930, **1**, 111–143.

Rock, I. The perception of direction in the visual field. Doctoral thesis, New School for Social Research, 1952.

Rock, I. The perception of the egocentric orientation of a line. *Journal of Experimental Psychology,* 1954, **48**, 367–374.

Rock, I. The orientation of forms on the retina and in the environment. *American Journal of Psychology,* 1956, **69**, 513–528.

Rock, I. *The nature of perceptual adaptation.* New York: Basic Books, 1966.

Rock, I., & Halper, F. Form perception without a retinal image. *American Journal of Psychology,* 1969, **82**, 425–440.

Rock, I., Halper, F., & Clayton, T. The perception and recognition of complex figures. *Cognitive Psychology,* 1972, **3**, 655–673.

Rock, I., & Heimer, W. The effect of retinal and phenomenal orientation on the perception of form. *American Journal of Psychology,* 1957, **70**, 493–511.

Rock, I., & Leaman, R. An experimental analysis of visual symmetry. *Acta Psychologica,* 1963, **21**, 171–183.

Rock, I., & McDermott, W. The perception of visual angle. *Acta Psychologica,* 1964, **22**, 119–134.

Rudel, R. G., & Teuber, H.-L. Discrimination of direction of line in children. *Journal of Comparative and Physiological Psychology,* 1963, **56**, 892–898.

Shepard, R. N., & Metzler, J. Mental rotation of three-dimensional objects. *Science,* 1971, **171**(3972), 701–703.

Sperry, R. W. Effect of 180 degree rotation of the retinal field on visuomotor coordination. *Journal of Experimental Zoology,* 1943, **92**, 263–279.

Steinfeld, G. The effect of retinal orientation on the perception of form. Doctoral thesis, Yeshiva University, 1968.

Steinfeld, G. The effect of retinal orientation on the recognition of novel and familiar shapes. *Journal of General Psychology,* 1970, **82**, 223–239.

Steinfeld, G., & Greaves, S. The effect of retinal orientation on word recognition. *Journal of General Psychology,* 1971, **85**, 245–257.

Stone, L. S. Functional polarization in retinal development and its reestablishment in regenerating retinae of rotated grafted eyes. *Proceedings of the Society for Experimental Biology and Medicine,* 1944, **57**, 13–14.

Stone, L. S. Polarization of the retina and development of vision. *Journal of Experimental Zoology,* 1960, **145**, 85–93.

Stratton, G. M. Some preliminary experiments on vision without inversion of the retinal image. *Psychological Review,* 1896, **3**, 611–617.

Stratton, G. M. Upright vision and the retinal image. *Psychological Review,* 1897, **4**, 182–187. (a)

Stratton, G. M. Vision without inversion of the retinal image. *Psychological Review,* 1897, **4**, 341–360, 463–481. (b)

Sutherland, N. S. Visual discrimination of orientation by octopus. *British Journal of Psychology,* 1957, **48**, 55–71. (a)

Sutherland, N. S. Visual discrimination of orientation and shape by the octopus. *Nature,* 1957, **179**, 11–13. (b)

Sutherland, N. S. Cat's ability to discriminate oblique rectangles. *Science,* 1963, **139**, 209–210. (a)

Sutherland, N. S. Shape discrimination and receptive fields. *Nature,* 1963, **197**, 118–122. (b)

Thouless, R. The experience of "upright" and "upside down" in looking at pictures. *Miscellanea Psychologia, Albert Michotte* (Editeurs de l'Institut Supérieur de Philosophie, Louvain). Paris: Libraire Philosophique, Joseph Vrin, 1947. P. 130.

Zusne, L. *Visual perception of form.* New York: Academic Press, 1970.

# Index

Numbers in *italics* refer to the pages on which the complete references are
listed.